Jazz Voices

Jazz Voices

Kitty Grime

Quartet Books
London Melbourne New York

First published by Quartet Books Limited
A member of the Namara Group
27/29 Goodge Street, London W1P 1FD

British Library Cataloguing in Publication Data

Grime, Kitty
    Jazz voices.
    1. Jazz music
    I. Title
    785.42   ML3506

    ISBN 0-7043-2390-7

Typeset by MC Typeset, Chatham, Kent
Printed and bound in Great Britain by
Mackays of Chatham Limited, Kent.

Acknowledgements

All material used in this book originated in long interviews conducted by Kitty Grime, with the exception of that listed below.

Connee Boswell (p. 42) quoted by John Lucas, 'Another Boswell Chronicle', *Jazz Journal*, January 1974; reprinted by permission of *Jazz Journal International* magazine
Hoagy Carmichael (pp. 35, 40, 41, 43, 45) from *Sometimes I Wonder* by Hoagy Carmichael (Da Capo Press, 233 Spring St., New York, NY 10013) pp. 204, 292, 268–9, 196, 202, 179; used by permission
June Christy (p. 77) from *Straight Ahead – the Story of Stan Kenton* by Carol Easton (Da Capo Press, 233 Spring St., New York, NY 10013) p. 110; reproduced by kind permission of the author
Miles Davis (p. 162) from *Jazz Rock Fusion* by Julie Coryell and Laura Friedman (Marion Boyars Publishers Ltd., London W1) p. 41
Duke Ellington (pp. 47–8) from *Music is My Mistress* by Duke Ellington (Quartet Books Ltd., London W1) pp. 123–4; used by permission
Babs Gonzales (pp. 107, 161, 169) from *I Paid My Dues* by Babs Gonzales (Expubidence Publishing Corporation, East Orange, New Jersey 07107) pp. 39, 122, 123
Lionel Hampton (pp. 36, 61) from *The World of Swing* by Stanley Dance (Da Capo Press, 233 Spring St., New York, NY 10013) pp. 275, 277; used by permission
W.C. Handy (p. 37) from *Ain't Misbehavin'* by W.T. Ed Kirkeby (Peter Davies Ltd., London WC1) p. 168; used by permission
Billie Holiday (pp. 34, 153–4, 155–6, 160, 161) from spoken introduction to 'Fine and Mellow', *Immortal Sessions Vol. One*, Saga Records 6905
Barney Josephson (pp. 155, 159, 162, 163) from interview with Derek Jewell, *Sunday Times*, 25 March 1973; used by permission

Barney Kessel (p. 49) from *From Satchmo to Miles* by Leonard Feather (Quartet Books Ltd., London W1); used by permission

W.T. Ed Kirkeby (pp. 37–8, 75) from *Ain't Misbehavin'* by W.T. Ed Kirkeby (op. cit.) pp. 177–78

Frankie Laine (pp. 72–3) from *52nd Street – the Street of Jazz* by Arnold Shaw (Da Capo Press, 233 Spring St., New York, NY 10013) pp. 151–52; used by permission

Mel Lewis (p. 89) from *Straight Ahead* by Carol Easton (op. cit.) p. 186

Anita O'Day (pp. 11, 60, 73, 93, 113, 140, 147, 148, 164, 180) from *High Times, Hard Times* by Anita O'Day and George Eells (Corgi Books, Century House, 61–63 Uxbridge Rd., London W5) pp. 96, 53, 43, 56, 69, 100, 53, 264, 278

Ann Richards (pp. 10, 88, 89) from *Straight Ahead* by Carol Easton (op. cit) pp. 183–84, 184, 184–85, 186

Max Roach (pp. 167–8, 177) from 'Behind the Beat of a Different Drummer' by Skip Laszlo in *The Wire*, 1982, pp. 22–23; used by permission

Artie Shaw (p. 155) from *The Trouble with Cinderella* by Artie Shaw (Da Capo Press, 233 Spring St., New York, NY 10013) p. 230; used by permission

Mel Torme (pp. 21, 48, 64, 103, 111, 113–14, 171) from interview with Brian Case; used by permission

Sarah Vaughan (p. 51) quoted by James Liska in an interview in *Down Beat* magazine, May 1982

Ralph Watkins (p. 163) from *52nd Street* by Arnold Shaw (op. cit.) pp. 212–13; used by permission

Teddy Wilson (p. 160) quoted by Don deMichael in his sleeve notes to *God Bless the Child*, CBS 66267

Lester Young (p. 99) from *The Jazz World* by Don Cerulli, Burt Korall and Mort Nasatir (Dennis Dobson Ltd., London W8) p. 89

Short quotations from Joy Marshall, Dorothy Donegan, Milt Hinton, Mel Torme, Roy Eldridge, Barney Kessel, Woody Herman, Duke Jordan, Urszula Dudziak, Jerry Wexler, Alan Clare, Ronnie Scott, Kenny Clare, from interviews with the author

Illustrations

Susannah McCorkle (*courtesy of Susannah McCorkle*)
Norma Winstone (*courtesy of Norma Winstone, photograph by Dennis Austen*)
Annie Ross (*courtesy of Granada TV*)
Pepi Lemer (*courtesy of Pepi Lemer*)
Marian Montgomery and Richard Rodney Bennett (*courtesy of Clarion, photograph by Reg Wilson*)
Johnny M (*courtesy of Johnny M*)
Adelaide Hall (*photograph by David Redfern*)
Digby Fairweather (*courtesy of Digby Fairweather, photograph by David J. Thomas*)
Sheila Jordan (*courtesy of Sheila Jordan, photograph by W. Patrick Hinely*)
Joe Lee Wilson (*courtesy of Joe Lee Wilson*)
Carrie Smith (*courtesy of Carrie Smith, photograph by James J. Kriegsmann*)
Trummy Young (*courtesy of Trummy Young*)
Cleo Laine and John Dankworth (*courtesy of the Dankworths*)
Jackie Cain and Roy Kral (*courtesy of the Krals*)
Barbara Jay (*courtesy of Barbara Jay*)
Bobby Short (*courtesy of Elektra Records, photograph by Anthony Edgeworth*)
Peter Dean (*courtesy of Peter Dean, photograph by Maurice Seymour*)
Marion Cowings (*courtesy of Wholly Cow Productions, photograph by Stephen B. Elliott*)
Elaine Delmar (*courtesy of Elaine Delmar, photograph by Danny Allmark*)
George Melly (*courtesy of Termag Limited*)
Georgie Fame (*courtesy of Ronnie Scott Directions Limited*)
Jay Clayton (*courtesy of Jay Clayton*)
Al Jarreau (*courtesy of Warner Bros Records*)
Ray Charles and Billy Eckstine (*photograph by David Redfern*)
Betty Carter (*photograph by David Redfern*)
Jimmy Witherspoon (*photograph by David Redfern*)
Leon Thomas (*photograph by David Redfern*)
Helen Merrill (*photograph by David Redfern*)
Marilyn Moore (*courtesy of Marilyn Moore*)
Slim Gaillard (*photograph by David Redfern*)
Mose Allison (*courtesy of Elektra/Asylum Records*)
Sylvia Syms (*photograph by David Redfern*)
Bobby McFerrin (*photograph by David Redfern*)
Beryl Bryden and Billie Holiday (*courtesy of Beryl Bryden*)
Joe Williams (*photograph by David Redfern*)
Ray Ellington (*courtesy of Ray Ellington*)
Charles Cochran (*courtesy of Charles Cochran*)

Contents

Introduction

Let me tell you about the very first jazz voice that fascinated me.

It was the first year that I had heard jazz, and I was in Paris, starving for the summer, and hearing my very first American jazz musicians – those were the days of the Musicians Union ban, which had been in force since the thirties, and stopped Americans playing here, and vice versa. Inez Cavanagh was a stout, middle-aged (to these teenage eyes) black American lady, who fronted a tiny fried-chicken place on the Left Bank. And every night she would lean against the wall in a pin spot and sing the great American songs, with a grave, long-fingered piano player called Aaron Bridgers. I had never heard songs like 'Lush Life' before and night after night I was fascinated. It was the tasty choice of words and music, the unlovely but moving voice, the off-hand but intense intimacy of the manner, the sympathy of the piano player, and the closeness of her grip on our attention. It left its mark.

It seems that, a lucky few apart, jazz singing is a thankless task. For most of the people in this book, the careers, the chances to do it come and go. Biggies apart – ask the man in the street for *that* handful of household names – there are the dozens of low-key, deflected, interrupted, flawed careers, no less dedicated. Yet, as I talked to those people; the fresh-faced, the fashionable, the ex-fashionable, the disappointed, the stickers, the resigned, the veterans, the philosophical alike, it was plain that the original impulse remains. And, first and last, the impulse is to get up and add your sound to what the jazz musicians are doing. That's what makes you do it, when you first summon up the nerve to do it. And the impulse stays, no matter what happens to the nerve. So this book is about the impulse and what happens to it, via hard starts, head starts, hits, high times, heart-breakings. And I've let the singers and the jazz musicians who play for them speak for themselves.

Here's how I planned it. I stayed out of the 'What's a jazz singer?' talk. I've tried not to be purist, racist, ageist or sexist. First, I made a list of people whose work has intrigued me. This included some who have amused, puzzled or disappointed me over the years. And some I admire mostly for their nerve and/or staying power. The list started short, got longer. Then I began the endless business of tracking them down. Then space, time and money ran out. So if your special favourite isn't here, or talked of, neither are a lot of mine.

I wanted to include the performance disciplines from cabaret to jazz places; the span of age and styles. Then I wanted to talk to jazz musicians who sing – my favourite singers – and players who spend most of their working lives with singers. I went to the local library for words from the departed and the un-get-at-able. So most of the people I wanted who couldn't or wouldn't talk to me are talked about. For, with all those letters, transatlantic calls, endless promises from public relations people, endless stalling from managers and other power maniacs, and all the hanging about, sorry about *you*, Ella, Sarah, Peggy, Tony, Lena, Blossom, Cab, Carmen, Ernestine, Alberta, you can't say I didn't try. Just be glad I didn't print everything they told me about you.

Some words about the ones who did talk to me: alphabetically, of course.

Player-singers – my favourite singers of all.

Chet Baker, whose scatting gets more moving as his trumpet chops come and go was talked into talking by a mutual friend – sorry I just didn't *have* that twenty-five dollars to give you, Chet. I was intrigued by Richard Rodney Bennett's determination to sing, with all his world of experience and success as composer and player in, out of, and around the popular music field. Barbara Carroll, an imperious, ladylike figure at the Carlyle Hotel's grand, a swinging pianist since bebop days, spoke of a start-out singer's vulnerabilities, bless her. Bill Dillard, a multi-faceted man, had his seventieth birthday cake on stage when I saw him in *One Mo' Time*. Ray Ellington, body-builder and entertainer, took no word I said seriously for a moment, just topped up the champers. Digby Fairweather loves songs, singers, singing and must be the most agreeable trumpet player to have with you on the stand. On stage, Slim Gaillard seems to wander bemused but twinkling between piano, guitar and mike, but don't let any of it fool you. Milt Jackson, still *the* vibes player for my generation, talks about singing each time I see him, and blushes. I always loved James Moody's tenor playing, but his scat singing is irresistible, and he gave me a mini master class: Moody, if ever you read this I *am* sticking out my stomach and holding those tones like you told me. George Shearing loves to sing – so that's what we talked about. The scathing things he had to say were emphasized by the softness of his speaking voice. Betty Smith is noted for her stomping tenor playing: so that wistful voice comes as a surprise. Most singers mentioned drummers as a major problem. So I tracked down the exemplary Grady Tate, who is a great drummer, survivor and a seductive singer to boot. And I snatched brief words with Trummy Young, that courtly veteran, at Kettner's.

Singer-piano players came next:

Mose Allison turned out to be every bit as aware, and as wry, as you'd think from his records. I was given fifteen minutes of Ray Charles's time. His heavies stood round making throat-cutting gestures just as the chat warmed up. I heard Charles Cochran on my very first night in New York this time. He has an infinite appetite for and taste in songs, and does them in a warm, understated way. He told me I must check out Bobby Cole. So I did, and that wry-mouthed performing mask intrigued me – his music opens up as the night wears on, but not his eyes. A cruel tease, Cole's talk with me was the most unguarded of all. Bob Dorough is a unique singer-player: and all the hip singers do his songs, too. Georgie Fame juggles pop, jazz and rock 'n' roll every night he's on – he's faithful to his feelings for good-time jazz, and he's faithful to the jazzers in his team. Dave Frishberg said some harsh things about singers, and now he's singing himself; I love every wilful note he does, and his songs as well. Shirley Horn must be *the* cult performer. A near-legendary figure, seldom seen outside Washington, she's just about everybody's favourite singer-player of all. Mike McKenzie holds elegant court at the Dorchester every night; he'll play your favourite tune and he turns on the heat when he can. Rose Murphy doesn't change – plays and chirps in that tinkling but tough as bone-china way, and talks with undimmed enthusiasm. Bobby Short, super-smart, supercilious, received me in his sombrely grand apartment opposite Carnegie Hall and yawned most of the time.

Accompanists:

Jimmy Lyon has played for countless singers in and out of jazz – I first heard him here with Mabel Mercer. He was at the Waldorf in NY, where Cole Porter's fruitwood grand gets top billing. 'Oh, well, back to the ironing-board,' he said, as we talked between his sets. Jimmy Rowles was here with Ella, and did his ten-in-the-morning best to be curmudgeonly with me, lovely man. He is specifically most singers' favourite piano player. I had to prise the chat out of Pat Smythe, though we all know he knew just what he liked. Bobby Tucker was here with Billy Eckstine, was with Billie Holiday in the forties. His pithiest comments came after I'd run out of tape. Mal Waldron lives and works mostly in Europe now. Apart from his own distinctive jazz style, he was Billie's last accompanist.

The other quotes from musicians have been in my files for years, waiting for the light of print.

Others:

Milt Gabler represents the record business, jazz and all (he has at least forty million-sellers to his credit). He's been in it and at it since the late twenties, first with the famous Commodore record shop, then the Commodore record label, then with more commercial concerns. He supervised countless classic jazz sessions: his taste, ear and musical memory are legendary. John Hammond's quotes are from a lecture I heard him give at St Peter's Church in New York. Joy Kane's lively Sing Jazz classes taught me more than I can tell you (but I could *show* you). Sal Mosca, a most dedicated, disillusioned piano player, carries on the demanding, idealistic methods of the Lennie Tristano school in his teachings. Rosetta Reitz is a committed feminist writer with a life-long passion for jazz. She has been finding, compiling and reissuing the work of many long-forgotten blues singers.

Singers:

First, the veterans. I was dazzled by the fun and games of Adelaide Hall, who relished the elegancies of Paris in the mad twenties, posh London in the thirties and still gets everyone going. And dear, sensible Helen Humes, who was very ill when we talked between sets at Ronnie Scott's, and died a few months later. I caught Maxine Sullivan, a spry, white-haired jenny wren of a woman at a Bronx jam session. Maxine had her hit in 1937, still makes every note she goes for and still makes the band swing. I heard Julia Steele for the first time with the Savoy Sultans. She's in the swinging tradition, has seen most of the usual career ins and outs, including a longish gap after a bad car crash.

From the cabaret edge of the jazz spectrum, I spoke to Elaine Delmar, Salena Jones, Marian Montgomery – how I admire their poise, their programming and the jazz nuances in their presentation. Peter Dean (an extraordinary and sprightly veteran), Johnny M and George Melly love to entertain with jazz, relish vintage sounds including the camper overtones.

Jimmy Witherspoon and Eddie Vinson spoke to me for the blues

– a book in itself, of course. Carrie Smith and Beryl Bryden carry the torch for the classic styles of the great blues singers – strength to them.

Then, for singers in the classic interpretative traditions: Julie Amiet came here from down under, made it (if several months at Ronnie Scott's is making it), and has just gone back, hopes dashed. Be back soon, Jules. I met Marion Cowings at a record session, heard him at a jam session, talked to him on a train from the Bronx down to Mott Street. He's a highly aware performer with the sleek looks of a twenties matinee idol. And every word he said was to the point. British jazzers told me young Carol Kidd sings as naturally as any bird. And she does. Susannah McCorkle, that pretty, and pretty determined, heiress to a great tradition, makes her way, and is getting her breaks, in NY these days. Sylvia Syms, a vivid, wordly woman, has been doing it since the forties with notable jazz sensitivity. I spoke to her in a crowded dressing-room.

I met cult ladies:

Abbey Lincoln, that fiery beauty, mesmerized me with her sound, dramatic gestures and sibylline pronouncements. Helen Merrill always had a unique and admired sound on records, part taste, part technology. Glamorous Marilyn Moore gets most of her bread as a psychologist these days. Both have always been admired by the jazzers, both were instantly friendly and forthright. And it's always a pleasure to talk to Annie Ross, who these days divides her time between acting and singing; but her jazz feelings are always there.

I talked to some of the out-and-out improvisers:

Mother figures Betty Carter and Sheila Jordan – both totally uncompromising, both knowing and feeling too much to play show-biz ego games. Father figures: Mark Murphy looked years younger and cooler than when I first heard him twenty years ago. Jon Hendricks – thanks for the tape. Jon is *the* influence on the younger ones – from Leon Thomas, Joe Lee Wilson to new excitement, Bobby McFerrin. Each of these men is an individualist, all are crucially entwined in jazz experiences.

More improvisers; inside and outside the free music scene:

Jay Clayton and Jeanne Lee are brave, helpful, resourceful stalwarts of the New York scene. Our own Pepi Lemer, Maggie Nicols (whose chat, of a staggering candour, has been somewhat pruned of names to protect the guilty) and Norma Winstone determinedly do their many things – why does Europe reward them more than we do? Flora Purim these days has a highly-polished-up Latin jazz thing – highly crowd-pleasing. I've talked to Anita O'Day twice – first time she got me drunk (I was quite young in this game), second time she walked out of the room after five minutes. So I had to go to her autobiog for most of it.

Combos:

Jackie Cain and Roy Kral are a groovy pair with American Dream looks and no-nonsense chat. I asked Sweet Substitute, that sequinned threesome, about their Boswell Sisters start-out – before *soul* took over.

Those who learned their craft with the big bands:

Rosemary Clooney, a warm impulsive lady, is today involved with the younger generation of mainstream jazzers more than ever before in her life. Chris Connor, shy but direct, still has her unique sound. Barbara Jay told me some of the trials of the fledgling band singer. Billy Eckstine and Joe Williams can certainly turn on the male charm, but talk straight down the line. Both make those concessions to pop tastes, but you can't mistake their jazz feelings and their rapport with jazz musicians.

Superstars:

Al Jarreau was on his way up there when I talked to him. He's made it in the commercial area, but it only proves the rule that jazz tastes are the most unsaleable side of any singer. Cleo Laine, superstar at last, not too soon or too late, talked to me back in 1976, and again last Christmas, superstardom whirling her all over the place in between.

But here's the thing that gave the edge to the enterprise. When I got together my last collection of conversations with jazzers, I hadn't made that step from listening to doing it. Now I have. ('Yes, I heard you'd started. Get in the queue,' said one of the singers crisply, as we chatted.) I won't bore you, as I do everyone else, with my growing-pains. Let's just say that I learned more on my first gig than in all those twenty-odd years of listening and talking.

This book reflects all of it. Because I know now what they're talking about: what gives you those sleepless nights, surges of paranoia, angry tears, depressions, those drudgeries, and praise be, that unpredictable, purest thrill – don't try it, you might like it, as they say.

So, love and thanks to all. It was a pleasure. Thanks to the Irvines in New York for patience and hospitality; to Howard Johnson and John McKellen for contacts; to Brian Case for loaning me his Mel Torme interview; to Phil Lee for checking some technicalities; and everyone else who has told it like it is.

1
Working

. . . they talk about it – the wheres, ways, whys and hows
of it . . .

They see you on the bandstand. But that's the end *result*.   LEON
THOMAS

You are a new bride every night. Is it going to be all right? Are they
going to like me?   BOBBY SHORT

Every time I get on stage, it's like I'm up there for the first time.
HELEN MERRILL

It's an act of seduction, as it were, absolutely. It's meeting strangers
and the unexpected happens.   BOBBY SHORT

You never know. Every place is different. Every audience is different. You never know.   JIMMY ROWLES

How *can* you know? I don't really know what I'm going to do until I
do it.   SYLVIA SYMS

You just, kind of, take off. And you don't know where you're going.
And you don't know where you're going to land.   MARILYN MOORE

I love that feeling – not knowing whether it's going to be good or
bad. Or if it's going to *happen*.   SHEILA JORDAN

God, it's *fun*. You didn't realize how much fun it is to *do*.   JOE
WILLIAMS

I love singing. It is such a *pleasure*. And you cannot say on an instrument what you can say vocally.   GRADY TATE

Sometimes you can reach up and get that rare moment. Yes, at some point in your performance each night, you can get that rare *excruciatingly* beautiful moment.   JOE WILLIAMS

Sometimes, it's just so easy. It's just not *me*, doing it. And it feels so *good*.   JAY CLAYTON

Once you've hit a peak, like, singing with the best people, you want to recapture the magic moments all the time.   JULIE AMIET

And you never know when the beautiful moments are going to happen. Because every musician wishes that every moment could be a beautiful moment.   JAMES MOODY

Really to get the intensity and the passion and the vitality and the energy, I think that's what it's about.   ANNIE ROSS

Because entertaining is like magic, you know. And we are the magicians. Music is magic.   JOE WILLIAMS

In the final analysis, it depends on how much magic you *have*.
ABBEY LINCOLN

We do a most exposing kind of music, you know. It not only puts your musicianship on the line, it puts your whole existence on the line.   MARK MURPHY

You might as well walk about butt-naked up there.   MARILYN MOORE

A jazz singer is more vulnerable in some ways, because you're interested in more things than seducing the crowd, you know. You have an obligation to the music, above your obligation to entertain your audience. I'm always more interested in my musicians, *their* acceptance.   HELEN MERRILL

Here's my business. Every day I get up and I go to the piano. And I start to practise. First, I get ready whatever I need for the night. I start at the *end* of the day. And then I sit down and practise. What do I practise? I practise *songs*.   BOBBY COLE

Sometimes a tune will be in my mind all day. Whatever I do, that one tune comes back and lays with me all day.   MILT JACKSON

I blossom through music. It makes me *live*.   SALENA JONES

8

Someone said to me, 'You look completely different when you sing, your face and your eyes. You become a whole different person.' I never forgot it.   MARILYN MOORE

That audience, they see me for the first time, for about a minute. And it may occur to them that I am elderly, or young. Or tall, or short. Or fat, or thin. Or whatever. But, after that moment is over, then who *I* am comes forward. And if that isn't enough to keep anybody busy and interested, then I have nothing going for me.
SYLVIA SYMS

You see people be transformed. People who are not beautiful *become* beautiful. The music does this. It does this to musicians too. You see tired sick old people become what they ought to be, what they want to be. Through the music. It's the holy spirit that comes. I can see the spirit on my face when I come from the stage.   ABBEY LINCOLN

Well, I'm having problems tonight. I'm having a throat problem. I'm having a cold problem. But all that will vanish when I get out there. I will feel no pain.   SYLVIA SYMS

I've worked when my body wasn't strong, when I was in pain. After I came off, I remembered, I'm infirm. But while I'm on the stage, I'm in another dimension. All my problems were gone. The spirit has power over the body. It *does*.   ABBEY LINCOLN

Sometimes the music can make you do it when you *can't* do it. That's the truth.   JAY CLAYTON

When you see me out on that stage, you will see me looking as good as it's possible to pull an old broad together. OK? And this person that you see being pulled together with *magic*, is not the person I am when I'm through working. I come in looking like some old bag lady.   SYLVIA SYMS

I like to feel *new* when I walk on stage.   SALENA JONES

I'm just keeping trying to dye my hair and staying as young-looking and sensuous as I can.   JIMMY WITHERSPOON

When I first came to New York, my manager said I must shave my beard off. Or he couldn't book me into smart clubs.   JOE LEE WILSON

Before the war, I used a grease you put on your head to have your hair straight, and it took the hair out. While I was waiting for it to grow back, I shaved it off, all of it. And people kind of took to it. So I thought, I'll keep it off, I don't need it no more. So, just a safety-razor every couple of days all over, *finish*, neat and clean. 'CLEANHEAD' VINSON

It's a nice feeling to be what you are. Some bandleader says to me, 'I got to go. I can't let anybody see any grey on my head. I got to go take care of that.' And I thought, maybe I better shave my beard off and get some hair colouring. And then they said, 'No, you'll lose your image.' SLIM GAILLARD

My looks? That's something Mom and Dad did. That's not anything I had anything to do about. But the singing . . . that I *had* something to do about. BILLY ECKSTINE

I tell them, 'This music is *elegant*.' When Jelly Roll Morton sat down at the piano, he was *attired*, diamonds in his teeth. People went to *see*. Billie Holiday always *dressed*. Bessie Smith – just look at her pictures. People went to see all that. People went to see that glamour and glitter. So I keep in the tradition of what I know about Bessie. What she did. And what she was *about*. CARRIE SMITH

A lot of groups say, 'Wear what you want and don't worry about a dress.' They come on in dungarees. But they *play*. I'm from the old school. For me to sing in dungarees, *well*. I'll tell you what happened to me in France. They lost my luggage and I had to go on that night in dungarees. It *killed* me. I got drunk. I had to get high to do it, I did. JULIA STEELE

You say you associate me with a glamorous image. This takes a lot of upkeep. I work in dinner-clothes, because it's simple. You find that if you can begin to pare things down to simplicity, then it's easier to get around to the complicated business of performing. So I work in a *uniform* – a dinner-jacket, and a fresh shirt for every show. BOBBY SHORT

A girl singer always had to look good, like she just came out of a shower. And that wasn't always easy to do. Sometimes the band would drive into a town and we wouldn't have time to check in, we'd go right to the job. I'd have my blue jeans on and my hair in curlers. I'd have to get my gown that was squished between the funky, smelly band suits, and grab my shoes and my overnight case and go in the ladies' room; the guys used the dressing-room, if there was one. I'd put my make-up on, take my hair down, change clothes while the girls were coming in in their dresses and corsages. I'd be

10

standing there putting my garter belt on – they really used to stare at me.   ANN RICHARDS

Oh, when you're seventeen, it's easy. You comb your hair, powder your nose, on you go. Later, it all takes a little longer.   HELEN MERRILL

To smile when you don't want to smile and to look bright and keep awake and be pretty when you don't want to – it's an ordeal. ADELAIDE HALL

I told Gene Krupa, 'But I'm not your ordinary peaches-and-cream band chick . . . I want to be treated like another musician . . . On one-nighters why can't I have a band jacket just like the guys, with a skirt to match and shirt?' It was as easy as that. I dodged dresses whenever possible. My uniforms became a kind of trademark . . . But after I invented the idea, it produced a lot of rumours about my sex life.   ANITA O'DAY

I played Carnegie Hall four, five times. And each time I felt better than the last. Because when I walked out on that stage, they just went, 'Aaaah!' I had half the battle won. They could say, 'Maybe she didn't sing good, but she sure looked good.'   CARRIE SMITH

When I started, you had to have some sort of sexual appeal, it was crucial. And it was a very stylized look – people were embarrassed by something unusual, I suppose. Today, it's pretty irrelevant. There are some *strange* singers, aren't there?   CLEO LAINE

Singers were done up in a very artificial way. You must remember Hollywood had a lot to do with that – the idea that women had to be *perfect* – the make-up job, the hair job, the glitter.   SALENA JONES

. . . long false nails, long false eyelashes, the lot, don't you remember?   ANNIE ROSS

One of the singers I've worked with wouldn't sing at a *party*, even, without her false eyelashes.   RICHARD RODNEY BENNETT

Oh, those terrible cabaret dates, when you're really getting dressed to go out and do *battle*. You had to do the full sequin bit. And I used to wear the wigs, and the diamanté earrings.   ELAINE DELMAR

Thank God for wigs. Wigs are an absolute godsend. I never have to worry about hairdressers, these days. Plonk on a wig, and people say, 'You look exactly the same as you did twenty years ago.'   BERYL BRYDEN

I always used to have a stage person, that I could hide behind. But I'm trying to strip that away more and more. I've become more aware of the two people, the *me* and the stage me. And I think I'm getting closer to *me*, now. I think I can almost be me. ELAINE DELMAR

To face an audience as you *are*, is much the most beautiful thing. But it takes time to find out what this *is*, this sense of yourself. MAGGIE NICOLS

I was idealistic at first, and thought, it's my *voice* they've come to hear. But when you go into the more popular field, as I've done, I can't get up there and *not* think about how I've made up my face and what dress I've got on. You've got to look like a somebody, like *you*, hopefully. You get to know how you want to look. And then you *maintain* that look.   CLEO LAINE

These days, a lot of young singers get their *look* together, before they get their music together.   JAY CLAYTON

You enhance the beauty you have within yourself. But on the other hand you can come on in a little black dress and knock them out. That happens, too.   SALENA JONES

Yes, *starving* in that little black dress.   JOY MARSHALL

What I am there to do is to let my light *shine*. I come to *appear* before them. And I do.   ABBEY LINCOLN

See what's happening now? Taking shape, aren't I? Not too glamorous, honey, it's not that kind of place. Casual. Hey, not *that* casual.   SYLVIA SYMS

I like to be comfortable, because I perspire more than I used to.   SHEILA JORDAN

One perspires. BOBBY SHORT

I know an audience loves to see you *sweat*.   MARILYN MOORE

I used to feel embarrassed about working so hard and perspiring so much on stage. But, since Lena Horne made it *chic*, I say, 'Let it all roll down.' SYLVIA SYMS

I have changed in broom closets, dressed in the dark. I know how to tie my bow tie in the dark. I have just slicked my hair down and walked on out there. And it doesn't change, you know. BOBBY SHORT

12

It hasn't changed since the days of Bessie Smith. There are magnificent places I've sung in, and I've had to walk through the kitchen, dodging all the desserts, before I go on.   CLEO LAINE

You never know when you go into a place, whether you're going to be treated like an artist, or the hired help.   CARRIE SMITH

★

Most of the preparation you need to do goes on in your mind.
NORMA WINSTONE

I like to get dressed very slowly. And put on my make-up very slowly. And I like to be in the theatre at least an hour before I have to go on. I like hearing the band warm up; that all means something to me, and somehow subconsciously gets me ready to work.
ROSEMARY CLOONEY

My therapy? I iron my own dress.   CLEO LAINE

I like to have my time to myself. Because when I go to the stage, I'll be alone. Even though there are other people on stage with me, we are all alone.   ABBEY LINCOLN

I meditate always before a concert. I think to nothing, zero out to nothing. It drives my wife nuts. 'What are you thinking about?' 'Nothing.' It makes you more *catlike*. A cat is totally relaxed, but in a split second can jump almost to the ceiling.   JOE LEE WILSON

I've sung under every possible influence, you know, being stoned, being drunk, all that. Now I never drink before a show, it's my discipline.   ANNIE ROSS

I know what *should* happen, preparing for an evening. But I've gone on sometimes when I've been so completely taken up with domestic problems and things, or things have gone wrong, and then you find yourself actually in front of a microphone before you know what's happened. And the words are, like, coming to you a split second before you actually sing them. It's quite frightening.
NORMA WINSTONE

The insecurity of performance is an inextricable part of performing, unless you sabotage your emotions by anaesthetizing yourself. The insecurity comes from having to throw yourself to the lions. It's do or die. It's love or be hated. In other words, you're putting yourself on the line. And you're up front. You haven't got an instrument to hide behind. Your body is your instrument.   MARION COWINGS

13

Didn't you notice last night, how quiet and nervous I was, smoking and all that? I'm still nervous, every time I go on. Every night for about three or four minutes, I'm a nervous wreck.   JIMMY WITHERSPOON

If you're nervous, then you have to work down. If you're *not* nervous, you have to work *up*.   MOSE ALLISON

I don't like to be on edge. Because, if I'm on edge, I have a tendency to *sound* on edge.   SHEILA JORDAN

Maybe the easiest time is when you've just started and you don't know what it's all about. You just go on and have fun. I've been in the business a long time. And I don't know if I'm more relaxed through experience, or if I worry more *now*.   ADELAIDE HALL

Early on I had to come to terms with embarrassment, as a fundamental fact of performing life. There is a certain amount to overcome in order to do it at all.   JOHNNY M

You can be shy and get the job done. Sometimes you have to be aggressive in order *to* get the job done.   BETTY CARTER

Well, *I'm* shy. One has to be a little shy. Because what you're doing is offering yourself – an intimate part of yourself – to people.   BOBBY SHORT

I *run* to the stage. I have to discipline myself not to just *give* myself away.   ABBEY LINCOLN

How do I like to *be* before I go on stage? I like to be *paid*. Preferably in advance.   LEON THOMAS

Look, this is your job. This is your living. And you've got to impress somebody, so you can get another job. Understand? You can't impress them by being *laid back* and *cool*. What's that supposed to mean? You can't be *laid back* on any job. If you're going to be *laid back*, you're going to be mediocre for the rest of your life. And you can't afford to let your musicians be *laid back*, either. If you're doing a job in front of people, your job is to please them.   BETTY CARTER

I had this problem when I first worked in restaurants, am I up front, or am I background noise? And I've since discovered that the brief for working in a restaurant is to provide wallpaper. But because one's ego is wrapped up in the whole business of performing that can be a tough pill to swallow.   JOHNNY M

14

Unless the sheer force of a singer's reputation can command an audience, it's very difficult, even for a very skilled singer, to get up in front of a brightly-lit roomful of people sitting eating and drinking, and command any attention.   DAVE FRISHBERG

Usually we start quietish, while they're having dinner. We creep up on them. We don't want them to have indigestion. We play nice and easy on the ear. On the second set, we open up a bit more. By that time, they're all stoned anyway.   RAY ELLINGTON

★

All an audience ever remembers is your opening number. And your closing number.   JOE LEE WILSON

You've got to get on. And you've got to get off. And in between, you don't want to stand up there and *die*. It's as simple as that.
MAXINE SULLIVAN

There are some songs that are wonderful openers – natural openers.
ANNIE ROSS

I start with a big one. A medium tempo swinger, with a big ending. The ending is rehearsed, but it's variable. No, it can't be a throw-away number. I very deliberately choose what I sing to introduce myself. Because I have to *get* them. And if I don't get them with my first number, by the second it might be too late. So it's most carefully thought out. It swings, mildly. It has lyrics that can be understood. I may scat a little bit, but I keep it short, no long solos. I try my best to involve the people, to win them. And gain their trust. I'm saying, 'Here's a man in front of you who's going to sing for you. You can trust him. And he can sing.' I want to get the audience *into* what's happening with me, through the music and my presentation. I choose a semi-familiar standard or a jazz standard, and work it into a jazz feel, and give it a big ending.   MARION COWINGS

I start the night *up*. Because if I start down, the show goes down, it seems to me. I start up and I try to stay up.   CARRIE SMITH

It's got to swing. I don't believe you've got to start with a big bang, as long as it swings. There's more impact in that than going on and blowing your head off.   BETTY SMITH

I don't like to go on and start up there. Because once you're up there, there's nowhere else to go.   CAROL KIDD

One thing I did learn very early on, mainly in the northern clubs here, was that if you sang rip-roaring, grab-their-attention-type songs, well, you *didn't*. Because they were so used to them, they'd talk through them. And drink through them. But if you started with a song that was low-key, they'd suddenly wonder what you were doing up there, not *singing*. I found the less you yelled, the more attention you got. So there were pauses and long gaps actually written into the music, so they just had to look at a face and a body. And I had to look as dramatic as I possibly could.   CLEO LAINE

I don't see why you shouldn't go on with a low-key opening number but, well, it's insecurity, I suppose. Perhaps singers feel it's easier to get through that first number, if it's a bright tempo. Perhaps your faults and your nerves don't show up so much.   NORMA WINSTONE

Billie Holiday would do it, go out there and start with something real soft and pretty, you know. And surprise them.   JIMMY ROWLES

You don't need to grab them by the throat. I think it's more like touching them on the cheek, instead.   MARILYN MOORE

I like to start off with something fairly cheerful. I like to show that I can sing, that I can play, and that they're going to enjoy what I'm doing.   DAVE FRISHBERG

I'm always a bit tense, because I've got so many things to think about out there. So I don't count it in, not the first number, because I get nervous and count things in *too* fast.   JULIE AMIET

The cabaret reason for starting with an up-tempo song was that people were looking you over. And it had to be a throwaway song to put them in a good mood. Then the second song was supposed to be medium groove. And then you could maybe get into some sort of ballad.   HELEN MERRILL

I might open with a free-form thing, singing and improvising about what I feel, I might open up that way.   SHEILA JORDAN

I just walk on and *my ears are behind me*. Listening to what's coming to help me do what I'm trying to do. Just as I get my inspiration from the musicians, I must inspire them as well.   SALENA JONES

I get out there and there's a certain spirit that overtakes me, a certain spirit of myself. If there's a big audience there, I try to make it come right into the centre, into a *one*. And, when I can feel them right into a one, then, I'm like, *open*, and I can do anything I feel. When the audience is with that spirit and I can touch them, through music, I feel it come back to me. You can feel a tremendous warmth sometimes, that makes them almost one person, one circle, one ball of love. They all come back to me like *one*.   SHEILA JORDAN

I always try to get through to the women as soon as I go on. The men are on your side, anyway. But if the women resent you, they won't let the men listen to you.   JOY MARSHALL

The women will talk all the time to distract the men from looking at you. Yes, I've seen them have hysterical laughing fits over nothing, all that. When I used to do all the glam sort of bit, I felt women hated me.   ELAINE DELMAR

Audiences were very difficult for me when I was young. I was sort of vulnerable and kind of pretty and I think I was resented by women in the audience. And looked at as a kind of sex object by the men. I underplayed my appearance purposely, coming from a Seventh Day Adventist background I thought it was sinful to wear perfume, even. So, for me, the exposure to all this harshness was very shocking. And it put me out of the business for a while.   HELEN MERRILL

And if you *don't* come on in a low-cut dress and all that, and the men are still interested in you because of what you're *doing* musically, some women seem to find this even harder to take.   NORMA WINSTONE

But you know what gets said to me every club I play? 'You're singing for the women.' If a man thinks you could be a threat to him, if his woman is looking at you – well, it's happened for hundreds of years, still happens. If you're a faggot, they'll let you make it.
JIMMY WITHERSPOON

I try not to look at people. I've been very put off when I've opened my eyes, and I see someone with what I think is a disapproving look. Or smirking to a friend, as I think.   NORMA WINSTONE

You can never tell whether people like you or not by the way they look at you. That's a mistake most singers make. I conducted a show at the Palace for Miss Garland (who was my favourite singer until I worked for her). And almost every night the people were on their feet, screaming, yelling. And this one night, *one man* didn't get up on his feet. And that's the one she saw. And singled out. And mentioned to me when I came into the dressing-room. And – get a load of this – she said, 'Why did they put that man right down front, where I could see him?' BOBBY COLE

I don't look at the audience. I don't try to sell the song. That's a separate art, almost, the selling of a thing. Like, being able to sing and put a smile on your face. Some singers can't get the smile off their face. I don't know how they can do that. And making all those movements with the hands to put it across. I don't know how they can do it. Billie Holiday didn't wave her arms about. CHET BAKER

As a child I was constantly singing, or day-dreaming. I always had my little world, you know. That's what I go into, when I sing. I had to learn to make it come *out*. Not just to do it for myself. Some-times, I have to remind myself right in the middle of a song, open your eyes and *look* at them. MARK MURPHY

I always watch faces. I watch faces with a theatrical intention, to involve the audience. I don't like to close off a fourth wall against them. I only do that if I'm telling them about an experience in a song, and I want them to be a sort of voyeur on me, and then I become a private person in a public place. MARION COWINGS

I like to see people smiling. But if you don't want to actually meet their eyes, you can look at a top button or a necklace, but everyone will think you're looking at them. BOBBY SHORT

Somebody taught me the trick of singing *past* people's faces. He said, 'You move your gaze around, but you're always focusing *behind* the people.' RICHARD RODNEY BENNETT

I focus more on the music than I focus on the audience. I don't spend too much time wondering what the people are thinking. That would get in the way. BOBBY McFERRIN

The secret is to get a good strong spotlight in your face. It takes all the shyness away. It makes the people just silhouettes, makes all the difference in the world. CHARLES COCHRAN

I like to start very bright. And then I like to stop and I like to speak to them and say that I'm pleased to be there. Not too much, of course. I'm wearing this big white fur, and I say, 'Let me get rid of this. I'm going to throw it in the wings. And if they don't catch it, I'll have to wash it again in Tide.' All these silly little things, you know. ADELAIDE HALL

I can't talk to audiences. There are some who talk more than they sing.   ELAINE DELMAR

For years I could open my mouth to sing, but I couldn't speak. I would think about announcing a tune, and I would rehearse to myself, '. . . and now, I'm going to sing . . .'. And I'd get up there, and I'd think, *now*. And nothing would come out.   NORMA WINSTONE

I don't know if you noticed, but a lot of my introductions are quite didactic, either historical or humorous, or both. At one time it was all improvised, but now if I hit a good joke I tend to keep it in.   GEORGE MELLY

I used to think, I'm a *singer*, not a compère or an announcer. But it's a big part of connecting with an audience. If things drop to the floor between numbers, you've lost your audience.   JOHNNY M

. . . now, *while* the audience is applauding, before they stop, I begin my second number, so there is no time for them to go back into their own world, their own conversation. I like to keep the thread of theatrical illusion going, in other words, to continue to suspend the disbelief. If, after the first number, they're still eating the chicken salad sandwich, I know I've got to take out my big guns again. And *get* them.   MARION COWINGS

I don't tell people how I put my thing together. That's my secret.
SALENA JONES

I'd say the pacing is forty per cent of the performance.   BOBBY SHORT

We have a sort of format that we've evolved over the years, although the songs change, of course. We figure out tunes that follow each other gracefully, different tempos, different keys. It bugs me to play three songs in a row in the same key.   ROY KRAL

I have a formula for my act now – but it's like a safety-net. I can give what I'd call a standard performance which is acceptable in front of a fairly indifferent audience. But no surprises take place. What I love is when the audience catches it and I catch them and it's a sort of exchange between us, which allows a certain wildness, both in the talk and the singing. Probably it's not all that different from the framework of the American jazz vaudeville. And the music hall of my childhood is as important.   GEORGE MELLY

I put songs together to make a mood. I have to have a thin psycho-logical story line going right through – a reason to get into and out of songs. And there's the right place to put a song. A song must be strong enough: there's a structure and a colour and a weight. MARIAN MONTGOMERY

There are lots of songs I love that can be beautiful in themselves, but not *work*.   ANNIE ROSS

Your real heavy listeners are the ones that stay on for the later sets. So I usually play the most easily accessible tunes early in the evening.   MOSE ALLISON

I programme by tempo. I sing something in contrast with what has gone before. We're dealing here with forty-five years of singing songs.   JOE WILLIAMS

I have to change the pace, manipulate the atmosphere with the lyric and song. That's what singing is about – it's a feeling thing.   MARION COWINGS

Sometimes I plan a set out, but lately I've just been calling the tunes. I like to plan things and then I like to leave it open, just to see what happens.   BOBBY McFERRIN

I do about twenty-four different songs a night and I shuffle them about a good deal, in fact every show I do, in order to make it interesting. A lot of singers don't do that. They repeat the same show more than once a night, assuming that the audience changes. CHRIS CONNOR

Sometimes I just call the key, beat out the time and take off.   ANITA O'DAY

Yes, I change my programme on the spur of the moment. I don't like to have tension on stage, so I try to talk the programme over in the dressing-room. I give them lead sheets for anything outside the standard jazz repertoire and a list of standard tunes and keys. If there's going to be any change in the agreed programme, I indicate it verbally, I turn quickly, *while* the applause is going on. You can have a problem if someone says, 'Don't know it. What else you got?'   MARION COWINGS

Sometimes, no matter how carefully you've prepared, it just doesn't work. Something happens in an instant and your mind says, no, I think I better do . . . and in that split second you do what your mind tells you. It's always good to follow your first mind. SALENA JONES

It's something I sort of *sense*. I *feel*, more than I hear, more than I see, the mood of the audience. MARION COWINGS

But you've got to make it look as if you're reading *their* minds, that you know what they want. And you say, 'Oh, *this* is going to get you.' MAXINE SULLIVAN

I want you to feel that you're at a big party. And each night something different is going to happen. CARRIE SMITH

But people feel secure with predictability – I'm sure there's an audience for it. They feel they're in control. MARILYN MOORE

People want to hear the songs you've recorded. And they want to hear it exactly as you did it on the record. HELEN MERRILL

After 'Loch Lomond' hit, I had to do it five times a night. Three or four songs, close with 'Loch Lomond'. And that went on for *years*.
MAXINE SULLIVAN

I *must* sing things like 'I Apologize' because that's why they *came*.
BILLY ECKSTINE

I was always surprised when Ella sang 'Lady Be Good' that it was always the same. She sang all the quotes on the record. And she said, 'Mel, people have become accustomed to it.' MEL TORME

Sometimes years later you have to learn your own record over again. ROSE MURPHY

I don't listen to myself. When I record a tune, I know I'm never going to sing that tune like that again. That's *over*. BETTY CARTER

I get new songs, but every place I go there come the requests for all the *old* things. HELEN HUMES

You can sing all the old songs but you can do them in a different way. In your own way. ADELAIDE HALL

I am very commercial-minded. Because unless you play music that you can eat by, you can't pay your bills. There's lots of beautiful *unknown* music. But unless it's been exposed, a lot of people tend to say, 'What is she doing?' and start talking to each other. SALENA JONES

Sometimes I'll be hollering changes at Bobby over my shoulder because I can see the jazz things are too hip for them. BILLY ECKSTINE

I used to put a current pop number, a good one, second in the programme, to catch all those people who don't like jazz. SUSANNAH McCORKLE

I play fashionable show tunes when people are coming in for cock-tails. I play for people who want to carry on a conversation. We get busier later on, and people want to listen. And then I start to *work*. People ask for tunes, I love playing requests. MIKE McKENZIE

Why I keep working, I don't know, but I don't take requests. I discourage requests, because most people's taste really *sucks*. BOBBY COLE

Sometimes you get a request for something you haven't thought of in a long time. And that will take you into a whole other area. BARBARA CARROLL

If everybody is hushed by the end of the first tune, if they are *into* me, if I've got them, then I can do a romantic song, speak to their hearts, instead of just their feet. MARION COWINGS

It's nice in a programme when you can indicate your vulnerability. I have an LP called *A Man Ain't Supposed to Cry*, and I get so many requests to do things from it. There are songs of tenderness, resignation, being rejected and what you feel about it. JOE WILLIAMS

At some point in the first set I let it go to an intimate level. I can only do that if I'm completely confident that the audience is on my side. I found this out the hard way. MARION COWINGS

I've done programmes which didn't work because I really didn't believe in what I was doing. And it came across. You've really got to be true to yourself. The whole programme is like a self-portrait. CAROL KIDD

Come and see a man wrestling with himself . . . MOSE ALLISON

It's easy for me to sing different lyrics about different emotions, because I experience hundreds of emotions in one day, God knows. MARILYN MOORE

The ending song has to be very important and big. So that there's an excitement generated, and when you leave, they say, 'Gee, I'd like some more of *that*.' ROY KRAL

I like to finish on something a little slow and sad, strangely enough. BETTY SMITH

I always end with the blues. Because the blues is the basis of jazz. JOE LEE WILSON

★

Talking to people between sets can break your concentration. Musicians have this problem too, not being allowed to *escape* in the break. NORMA WINSTONE

The worst thing about being a performer, I suppose, is that you live in a glass house, so to speak. Your privacy is very shaky. RAY CHARLES

Well, everybody *is* watching you, you know, if you're well known. So, when you come off, people are double-taking on you all the time. Yes, many performers are very shy. Ella is shy. Sarah is shy. But Dinah Washington wasn't shy. I'm not shy. BETTY CARTER

Crazy people come up to you all the time. People seek me out. And grab me during intermission. And tell me their problems. I'm at a very easy place to get to. BOBBY COLE

I like meeting new people and talking to people. It bothers my wife, though. AL JARREAU

I've even had people come up and start a conversation when I was on the stand and someone was soloing. NORMA WINSTONE

It's not that I'm like a priest in the confessional, but I'm the locum. BOBBY COLE

If people are drunk enough, crazy enough, they're determined to come up, to touch you, to talk with you while you're performing. BOBBY SHORT

It's a victim seeking another victim. I'm showing my feelings, so they think I'm a victim. And, of course, you're often showing something you don't know you're showing. BOBBY COLE

I only know that when the moon is full you get some funny people out. Boy, when the moon is full, they all come out. JULIA STEELE

The way a place presents you can make a big difference to the way the audience feels about you.   CHRIS CONNOR

The first ten years I was doing this, I was doing it in spite of the audience, usually. So I developed techniques for ignoring the audience, without being overt about it. And one of the things I came up with is that you don't play for a particular audience, you play for the universe. Just think of the galactic swirl going round, you know. I once imagined that if I played well and sang well it had the effect of counteracting ozone depletion, or something.   MOSE ALLISON

I think that, in order to entertain people, and in order to command attention from a room full of people, you've got to have, whether you're aware of it or not, an inbuilt *power*. You say, 'I'm going to take over. I'm going to do this with such *conviction* . . .' and that conviction comes and goes, doesn't it?   ANNIE ROSS

And the other trick is that you imagine there's one sympathetic person there at the back somewhere, who's *listening*. Another of these *myths* that gets you through the night.   MOSE ALLISON

I've given myself psychology about singer's paranoia. I don't like to make myself unhappy. I tell myself that people are there certainly for other reasons than just to hear me.   CHARLES COCHRAN

The whole life thing is going on there in a saloon.   MARION COWINGS

I've had people come in *defiantly*. And sit there and turn their heads away. Or look at you as if it's 'Well, how *dare* you? How dare you think you're so grand, up there.'   BOBBY SHORT

In a party of people there's probably only one that really wanted to come and hear you sing. The others talk all the way through the performance, quite oblivious of the fact that you're pouring your heart out, or trying to.   CLEO LAINE

I really hate it when somebody sits right under me and starts talking shop or something, right *under* me. I just *look* at them, real hard. And they get the message. Because I must look *evil*.   HELEN HUMES

It works to get softer and softer, if you can maintain your cool that long.   SHIRLEY HORN

I mean, the louder you sing, the louder they're going to talk.   CAROL KIDD

24

And you've got to be sure that what you were doing didn't give them a *reason* to talk.   BETTY SMITH

Every once in a while I'll say to them, 'Gee, can you hear me? Because I can hear you *good.*'   HELEN HUMES

I once said, 'Thank you, ladies and gentlemen. I call you ladies and gentlemen, but you know what you *are.'*   ABBEY LINCOLN

If I said something, and they answered me back, I'd be terrified, in case it might start a fight or something.   CAROL KIDD

I just do the show, say 'Thank you', and leave.   CHRIS CONNOR

I prefer it when other customers in the audience want to tell people to shut up.   BARBARA CARROLL

You can't *enforce* your own sense of decorum.   MARION COWINGS

I occasionally just stop playing until it quiets down, but I don't like to verbalize it.   BARBARA CARROLL

I've seen so many big-name singers act so bitchy and tough that they turn off the whole room. Then *nobody's* with them.   SUSANNAH McCORKLE

Billie Holiday wouldn't let people talk when she worked. When she was on stage, she commanded the stage.   ABBEY LINCOLN

It's not easy to command from the piano stool.   DAVE FRISHBERG

It's not easy to call the Muse. Under *any* conditions.   LEON THOMAS

I've felt like coming off in tears – of *rage*, you know.   JULIE AMIET

Oh yes, I've gotten angry. The worst time was in Eddie's Jazz Room, Kansas City. I'll never forget it as long as I live. It was a Monday night, and there was hardly anybody in the club. But right in front of me was one long table with about ten or twelve people. I came on and started to sing. And they were talking and talking. Fair enough. I always open with a fast one, so it was all right. Then there was the medium-bounce tempo thing. More raucousness. And then there was the ballad. At that point you know you're not going to get any attention, so you do your best. So I just got on with it. First two or three words and a fellow gets up, puts his foot on the stage and says, 'Hold it. Hold it.' I thought, oh, what's happened. The light was in my eyes, and I really couldn't see him. But he just waves his arms. So I stopped, and I said, 'What's the problem?' And he said, 'I've got to tie my shoe.' So I said, 'Ladies and gentlemen, let's indulge this gentleman . . .' And waited. And kind of laughed. He sat down. I started the ballad again. And all of a sudden he jumped up again. And I just lost my temper and said, '*Sir*. Everybody knows you're here. We *all* know you're here. The light is shining off your bald head.' And this woman jumped up and said, 'Don't you dare insult my husband. It's his birthday.'   MARIAN MONTGOMERY

Yeah, these music-loving audiences, they wouldn't know a flatted fifth, but they sure know how to diminish a fifth.   DOROTHY DONEGAN

I've walked away into the dark and turned my back on them and made a big silent scream, you know, made a terrible face. And then turned around, and *smiled*, you know.   CAROL KIDD

Mel Torme told me a marvellous story. Well, he's got a short fuse like me. He was in a club and he was doing his act. And this guy out front was *loving* it. Oh, he just loved Mel. And every time Mel did anything, he'd shout, 'Yeah, tell 'em, Mel baby.' And he wouldn't stop. And after the show, this idiot makes the mistake of coming backstage. And Mel recognized him. And the guy goes on, 'Oh, you're so wonderful, just wanna say how wonderful . . .' So Mel sits him down on a chair, and says, 'You really enjoyed it, did you?' And the guy goes bla bla bla. And Mel slaps him. And the guy is shocked. And Mel just says, 'Oh, so you really liked the show? What was your favourite song?' And the guy goes bla bla bla. And Mel slaps him again. And the guy jumps up, really mad. And Mel says, 'Listen Charlie, that's what *you* just did to my show out there.'   MARIAN MONTGOMERY

★

What's a good night? When the audience responds to what you're doing – that's a good night.   BETTY CARTER

When you come off and the audience has enjoyed it, there's no words for it. You just come off and you go 'Oooooh'.   ROSE MURPHY

I know when I've had a good night and the band's had a good night, because everybody rushes off stage and hugs each other and says, 'Wow, wasn't that *fantastic*?' And the night seems to go by so quickly. And everybody's just full of energy, you've got energy to *burn*. When you feel drained of energy, you know something's

wrong. And when it's bad, we just walk away from each other.
JULIE AMIET

It's funny how some nights it jells, everything. And some nights it's very hard graft.   ELAINE DELMAR

It's terrible when things don't work. It's like a broken love affair, awful. I suffer terrible when I've had a bad night. It's like a lovers' quarrel, no, worse, *worse* than a lovers' quarrel, awful, awful.
SHEILA JORDAN

If I find my mind wandering, I worry about it. I come off feeling how slack I am. And I come home and worry about it.   JULIE AMIET

If I'm not happy with the music I can't sleep. If it doesn't set right, if I can't strike the groove, I can't be bothered with anyone.   SHIRLEY HORN

If I do not control my feelings, it would be easy for me to suffer the things you suffer when you don't control what you feel. You suffer depression. Or exhilaration that's not real.   ABBEY LINCOLN

I just try to please and if I don't succeed, well, then, I'm sorry. I mean, they're not going to drive me to drink and drugs.   HELEN HUMES

I come here to perform. If you like it, fine. If you don't, the door swings both ways.   BOBBY COLE

Sometimes I think I've had a terrible night. And people will come up and say they enjoyed it. And sometimes, when *I* think I've sung really well, no one will say anything.   JULIE AMIET

If you've done a performance that doesn't meet your standards, all the applause in the world isn't going to make you feel good. Like pouring perfume on a *goat*, it makes it *worse*.   BOBBY COLE

Sometimes you'll try too hard, and there is such a thing as trying *too* hard, because you want to do so *good*. And you try so hard it just *bombs*.   JACKIE CAIN

We refer to it as 'spilling your guts'. Sometimes you feel you've just got to make *something* happen.   ROY KRAL

I had a quartet in San Francisco. And while somebody was taking a solo, I would leave the stage, go back into the kitchen and I would have some cake mix all set ready to go. And I would run out with the mixing-bowl and spoon, and go up on the stage and start mixing up a cake, run behind the bar and get a little vodka, gin, whatever, and put it in the cake. And then I'd run back in the kitchen, put it in the cake pan, throw it in the oven, come back and do my solo. Then, later on, I'd run and get it out the oven, bring it on the stage, put on the frosting, put a cherry in the centre, put little drops of bourbon – all the customers waiting to get a piece of the cake. I used to do all kinds of crazy things, for fun. But I mellowed down. SLIM GAILLARD

In my younger days, I went through the stage of despising audiences. That was before I understood that it's a tough job to *be* an audience. You see, everyone wants to be a star. MARION COWINGS

You cannot expect excellence every day of your life, no one can. But no matter how bad things may get, you know certain things will *work* for you, regardless. So if one night your mind is not as creative as you want it to be, you let that night go. If you are professional, even if you are having a low moment, the public won't know it. RAY CHARLES

So you have to get down to a certain rat-tat-tat, a certain precision, that takes you through every situation. BOBBY SHORT

Sometimes you could say it's almost like *copying* your best moments. ANNIE ROSS

Sometimes it seems you're going to work in a factory and you got to take care of your job. You may be a mechanical man up there, sometimes. SLIM GAILLARD

I saw Lena Horne at Las Vegas. And when the show was over, I said, 'You were just magnificent.' And she said, 'Oh, no. That was just a show, Bobby. When you just go on. And you sing the songs. And you bow. And the audience applauds. And that's all that was. Just a show.' And I learned that from her. That there are nights when that's all it is. You do a show. Because the audience does not give you anything more than just a space and a time to do that show. BOBBY SHORT

In my head, an entertainer plays the audience. Whereas an artist plays *himself*, his art. MARK MURPHY

Forget the bad things. Remember the good things. Then at least when you go you can say, 'Yes, it was good *once*.' MAXINE SULLIVAN

Some people love you. And some people really hate you. And some people just couldn't care less.   ABBEY LINCOLN

Let's face it, it's a business. If the people stay and order some more drinks, you've *won*.   CHARLES COCHRAN

A game, that's how I think of it. And if you win, you get to sing your songs, your way. And you get paid for it. And you can keep on doing it. And you can devote your time to getting better.
SUSANNAH McCORKLE

I was at the Vanguard one time, working opposite Miles Davis. Opening night, I was scared to death. All those people out front, all the best musicians in the world, there to see Miles. I'm in the back room behind, scared to death, 'What am I going to *do*?' And the guys said, 'Just kick ass, baby. *Kick ass*.'   SHIRLEY HORN

2
Who? And Where?

. . . they talk about some of the great jazz voices, some
of the great jazz times, and some of the places where
great jazz happens . . .

That's where it all began. In the church.   'CLEANHEAD' VINSON

I often think about how the gospel, spiritual music started. It's like a
good thing happening from a bad thing. Because the slaves in
America didn't have any musical instruments. They were forbidden
to play drums. They were forbidden to play anything. But when
they slipped off, they'd clap their hands, and they'd sing, 'Yes,
Lord, I'm going home, I'm going home some day. Yes Lord.' And
this clapping, this beat, is the basis of all the rhythm we use in
modern-day music that isn't symphonic or chamber music. That
beat. It started with the hands. Out of this grew this multi-million-
dollar industry. And jazz.   BILL DILLARD

In the church you were free to express your feelings in your voice.
No shame. You just let it all out. It was the only place you could be
expressive.   'CLEANHEAD' VINSON

These people would get up and whenever the spirit, as we say,
moved them, they'd react to it. Spontaneous. That's where I got *all*
the feeling, all of it, not some of it.   MILT JACKSON

And it seems that black people, for some reason or other, seem to
have a natural mechanism for singing. Many of our greatest singers
came from that particular religious background. They don't have
any training, many don't read a note. They *sing*. They don't know

31

anything about the proper production of the sound, but when they want to sing high, they just sing high, and when they want to, they can sing low.   BILL DILLARD

There used to be a programme on the radio called 'The Sheep and the Goats'. Viola Wells, 'Miss Rhapsody', told me. The sheep were the gospel music people and the goats were, of course, the blues singers. And there were so many complaints that the two musics didn't go together that they took the show off the air. Church people are very funny people. They're a little better now, but back then it didn't mix, blues and gospel.   CARRIE SMITH

People who were that religious were taught that the *other* music was sinful. Blues was the same music, but it was done in places the church people disapproved of.   MILT JACKSON

I'd always thought the blues and spiritual were close – close musically, close emotionally. And I was happy to hook 'em up.   RAY CHARLES

Ray Charles is all black music rolled up in one, forwards and backwards.   ROSETTA REITZ

Mahalia Jackson, she wouldn't sing the blues. But all she sang was blues all her life. Only the words were different. Because blues singing and spiritual singing is all the same if you compare the music. Mahalia mentions on one of her album covers that Bessie Smith's records were in her home, just like they were in mine. CARRIE SMITH

I think Dinah Washington brought the church to the nightclub. She would *preach* 'What a Diff'rence a Day Made'.   GEORGE SHEARING

I don't like that. There's times and places for everything.   HELEN HUMES

Spirituals were all about Africa – 'going home'. The blues is the same song, except that the words aren't about God, but human beings. The early country blues people just played any number of bars until they felt like making a change.   JOE LEE WILSON

They might do a six-bar, then a five-and-a-half-bar phrase. They were just singing what's coming to them, you know. 'CLEANHEAD' VINSON

But a standard form came up of twelve bars. Out of this grew jazz.   JOE LEE WILSON

I'm from Savannah, Georgia. Yes, I heard a lot of blues singers where I came up. I guess a lot of it was evolving into what we hear today. The people I knew who were singing the blues, they weren't names, they were the people who worked tapping the turpentine trees, and they would sing the blues in the evenings. They didn't work at it, they did it for their pleasure.   TRUMMY YOUNG

I remember first hearing the blues as a child back in Mississippi. This particular area had ten blacks to every white, and just about every store had a juke box: Memphis Minnie and Big Bill Broonzy. And it also had Glenn Miller and Tommy Dorsey.   MOSE ALLISON

The blues is a lifetime business.   JIMMY WITHERSPOON

The black theatres, that's what I remember when I was eleven, twelve. Every Saturday matinée I would be in the Standard Theater in Philadelphia, sitting right next to a wonderful trumpet player, Clarence Smith, who was my idol for many years. I saw the shows. I heard singers, Bessie Smith, Mamie Smith, all of them. I heard them all.   BILL DILLARD

Certain things seem to *come* to me. I don't know if it's reincarnation or what it is, but certain of the old musicians – like Jo Jones, he knew Bessie – have told me that when I sing they can *see* Bessie. There is a certain air about me.   CARRIE SMITH

I have all of Bessie on tape. I have them in my bedroom. And I go through them, from the first to the last, in order. Day after day. And I listen. And I find it a restorative. And a start to the day. I find it feeds me through the day.   GEORGE MELLY

Bessie Smith was a big, strong, strapping lady. And she could fill a theatre with her natural voice, no amplification. She could sing any kind of song. She did, of course, many humorous kinds of songs. She would open her act many times singing that we call an up-tempo song, a very bright lively tempo. She would sing a chorus of a song, and then she would narrate a whole monologue, say, of the man she was singing about who was mistreating her. And, of course, she quite often got the response of the ladies in her audience. She'd say things like, 'Now, girls, these men out there, they ain't worth a *dime.*' And the women in the audience would say, 'Yeah, you're *right*, honey.' And she would say, 'You treat them right, you turn around and they done slipped off with some other *gal.*' And she'd get another response. And she'd go on, and the orchestra would continue until she was ready to sing again. Most of the songs were very down to earth and related to true situations in the audience. The songs were saying what people were thinking.   BILL DILLARD

Bessie Smith, she had her ups and downs. She lived it, she lived the blues. That was her *life.*   'CLEANHEAD' VINSON

A lot of people think I'm a blues singer, but I don't think I'm a blues singer. I wasn't no young chicken when I joined Basie, you know. With Basie, Jimmy Rushing used to sing all the blues.   HELEN HUMES

Jimmy Rushing could generate the music. He made the music *happen.* And I think that's what good singers do. How did he do it? He'd just announce the tune, tell you the key, then he'd count it off.   DAVE FRISHBERG

When I first came to England with the Basie band, they'd write, 'Much of the enthusiasm was reserved for a singer called Joe Williams, who is no Jimmy Rushing.'   JOE WILLIAMS

And when I sang with Basie, they used to say, 'Well, he's no Joe Williams.'   LEON THOMAS

The traditionalists, they like what they *know.*   JOE WILLIAMS

I started singing in the little intervals when I was in a band, just to keep the thing going. And I would sing a little blues. And I just kept on singing.   'CLEANHEAD' VINSON

The blues to me is like being very sad, very sick, going to church, being very happy. There's happy blues and there's sad blues. The blues is a sort of a mixed-up thing, you just have to feel it.   BILLIE HOLIDAY

Anyone who sings must make their own blues. B. B. King, Joe Turner, Big Bill, they all have their own blues. You make things out of your own life.   'CLEANHEAD' VINSON

I like *happy* blues, you know. I don't like that down in the dumps and crying and sighing and moaning blues. I like blues like 'Million Dollar Secret' that make you laugh. The blues is so many moods. I just don't get into that *moody* mood.   HELEN HUMES

I don't sing the blues where you've *suffered.* It sounds funny to me to sing someone else's misery. I couldn't sing about the bossman doing this or that to me, working on the levee. Not even the pains of love, no, no, not for me. Most of mine have a little realism in them, but I'd rather make people laugh.   'CLEANHEAD' VINSON

In the beginning, I thought I didn't have to do the blues. I rejected being called a blues singer. Then I got mad because I read something Joe Williams said about not being a blues singer but a ballad singer. I got mad at him denying the blues at that time. And I thought, what about yourself? I thought, I don't sing any blues, either. So I decided I would sing a blues every time I performed. JOE LEE WILSON

If anyone thinks the blues is old hat, they're talking about cultural genocide.   LEON THOMAS

The blues transcends any race or religion. A lot of people have said it, but I feel that the blues is truth, you know.   MOSE ALLISON

★

I was always inspired by the horn player who sings, that was what got me into it, you see. Musicians who sing are a special breed. And you're damn right, it's closer to jazz.   BOB DOROUGH

Louis Armstrong was the idol of every trumpet player of his time, even as a singer. And, Lord knows, Louis had one of the most horrible sounding voices. But it was so beautiful.   BOBBY TUCKER

Louis Armstrong *was* a sound.   BOBBY COLE

I heard him in the late twenties. I enjoyed the *feel* that he had in his voice.   TRUMMY YOUNG

Louis went over to the Vendôme, Chicago, and became the singing actor, the shouting, moaning voice projecting over the hot horn and the ever-ready handkerchief. Using the big scarred lip, the smile that was to make him as famous a reciter-singer as a horn player. It's amazing the way he did it, the way he handled himself, a performance that was never ham. The guttural laugh, the husky moaning, the scatting of the words into incoherent patter. Behind it all was the horn playing, and that never let down.   HOAGY CARMICHAEL

Everything that Pops did, I think, was part of the show. Everything. From his handkerchief, to his eyes, to the total animation of the face, to the genius with which he played his instrument.   GRADY TATE

Louis did pop tunes of all sorts, but he always *crystallizes* it into some sort of jazz art, I think.   BOB DOROUGH

Louis is untouchable. He always had perfect time, tuning, a marvellous ability to bend a phrase so it was unmistakably a jazz phrase. And total originality, of course. And something that seems to have sunk without trace in jazz now, and that's humour. He sings and plays with all his heart. And it transcends the vehicle.   DIGBY FAIRWEATHER

How about Louis singing 'It's a Wonderful World'? When he sings that it warms my heart. It has so much poignancy. You can hear him saying 'It *is* a wonderful world, in spite of . . .'. He's just reminding us that underneath all this mess, it's a wonderful world. If you can put that into even the most platitudinous material, it's a brand-new thought again.   JEANNE LEE

Hollywood tried to make a buffoon out of him – I didn't think that was nice, either. I often wondered if he minded doing all that. We didn't dare bring it up. I don't know if he did it to go over bigger, or make more money. Because, in the earlier days, he just played jazz and he never seemed to have made much money doing it. Maybe his manager encouraged him to do it. It's unfortunate that so many people – *most* people – think of him from that point of view. But we musicians knew better.   TRUMMY YOUNG

Who knows what Louis Armstrong really thought? That's the way you had to *be* if you wanted to keep the job. Or *get* the job. That's the way it was, for many, many years.   BILL DILLARD

Earl Hines is right when he says that the people in the bands were the first 'freedom riders'. The black experience in music was a matter of heartaches, going hungry and even being beaten.   LIONEL HAMPTON

I remember those days. And I lived through them.   BILL DILLARD

You sang to get the gig. They'd say, 'You got a singer with the band?' 'Sure.' Oh, we can always come up with a singer, right? One of the jazzmen can sing. Something to fill the shoes.   BOB DOROUGH

I know a lot of them – interesting musicians who sing.   HELEN HUMES

Trummy Young is one of my great influences, speaking of the voice.

I used to love Lunceford's band, because I was also a jazz musician. And there was Trummy doing little speciality numbers and trios with the other guys. Things like 'Margie'.   BOB DOROUGH

I'm not a *singer*, I'll start with that right away. I don't have a voice for *singing*. I consider myself more or less as a stylist.   TRUMMY YOUNG

Whether they have a voice or not, musicians have a sense of phrasing, when they sing.   GEORGE SHEARING

I play the trombone because it's the nearest thing to the voice. I could hear the *voice* when I played it.   TRUMMY YOUNG

Jack Teagarden was a sort of brother of Louis, wasn't he? Definitely a great player-singer.   BOB DOROUGH

Any number of good players can sing. Jack Teagarden for one, he had his own way of doing it.   TRUMMY YOUNG

I think if you're a jazz person, you can play anything and make it work. Fats Waller is a good example. He could take a daft number and make it swing like the clappers. And put his own slant on a sentimental tune, make it funny as well. That was what endeared him to me.   RAY ELLINGTON

Fats Waller was a wonderful musician. Whenever he sat down to play, music just flowed out.   ROSE MURPHY

Fats came to London just before the war. He was adorable, everyone loved him. He couldn't have cared less about money, he just loved playing for people. His manager had to keep after him all the time. The night before he went home, he came down to the club and played. And the people stayed and stayed and went straight out to their work in the morning. And his manager was having a fit, saying, 'He'll never make the train, he'll never make the boat.'   RAY ELLINGTON

What a performance! Just imagine Fats sitting there with all this crowd around him, playing some out-of-this-world melodies. He would lift his right hand to take a draught from the glass of gin on the side, laughing at someone's joke, a cigarette perched on his lip, then without losing a beat or bar of melody, back to the drink again, and another draw at the cigarette, and a few more wisecracks. What co-ordination!   W. C. HANDY

Fats was many things to many men – you will have heard much of this man and his music. To you, he will be perhaps a gravelly voice on a record; a patron saint of a whole school of pianists; the composer of your favourite song; a buffoon who led a jumping group of jazzmen in monstrous sessions; or he may even be to you, by chance, a giant among jazzmen, whose recordings with his little band can lift you to the heights of ecstasy. Or maybe your position will lie somewhere in between all these? But whatever your position, it is surely not a negative one. No one has ever said, 'I can take Waller or leave him.'   ED KIRKEBY

Then, of course, my next influence was Nat 'King' Cole. He was such a unique pianist that you could be almost sorry that he sang, in a way.   BOB DOROUGH

Why did he decide to sing? Because he could make more money as an intermissioner, that's why.   SYLVIA SYMS

And he's singing and he's smiling, and it's one little hook on commerciality that enables the band to thrive. Then he becomes a big star – an industry.   BOB DOROUGH

Nat Cole was my first idol. When I started listening to the be-boppers, I liked Thelonious Monk and John Lewis. Then I started listening to a lot of classical sonatas. So what I'm doing now is a conglomeration of all that.   MOSE ALLISON

Nat Cole had a lot of taste. He never sang anything that sounded bad to me.   JEANNE LEE

A lot of drummers in those days would sing. There were a lot of guys that were, like, pimps. They didn't play good drums, but they were good-looking guys, and they wanted to hang around clubs where they could meet these chicks and do their business with them. They would sing a song and snap a little on their drums, and they would look all sharp and pretty and they'd get to meet the ladies that way. So Cab Calloway gets to be one of those kind of guys – he was good-looking and his sister was a star with her own band, so that's how he got in there.   MILT HINTON

Cab had his original style that was very successful and people loved it. 'Hi de hi, ho de ho', that type of thing, he had the whole world doing it. I think he was trying to reach the people, which he did.   SLIM GAILLARD

You always had musicians who sang, but you had very few male jazz singers. The only one, really, in the early days was Red McKenzie, who came up with the Chicago guys. Often, with the big bands, the boy singer sang the ballads, and some instrumentalist did the hot numbers or the novelties.   MILT GABLER

★

You know, in the twenties the women *reigned*. Women reigned in American music for that one decade. In the twenties women really had their act together. Most of them wrote their own material. There arc so many women who recorded over a hundred songs who are totally unknown now. It's hard to ignore these women. But they are ignored because the historians – mostly male, of course – were looking at the instrumentalists, listening to the instrumentalists. For instance, when Louis Armstrong was with Fletcher Henderson in 1924, he was the third cornet player. And he was picked to back singers on record dates, the way all the good guys were. Now, you can't tell me that when Louis was in the studio with someone like Bessie Smith, it wasn't Bessie Smith's *date*. He was a sideman and she was an important person. He did what she wanted. He had to. Now many of these singers' records have been reissued as *Louis Armstrong* records. What I am trying to do is put the women back in the perspective they should be in. Because seventy-five per cent of the so-called race records issued were blues and songs by women. ROSETTA REITZ

Race records? That was the name they gave to records that were made for the black people, mostly in the big cities. If you were white you probably never knew they existed.   BILL DILLARD

To me, the history of American popular music is an intermingling of black and white. For instance, Ida Cox, as a fourteen-year-old child in 1904 was in a minstrel show – a black woman in black-face. Thirty years later she was billed at the Apollo Theater in Harlem as 'The Sepia Mae West'. Now, Mae West had studied these black women's methods, and she was imitating their sound and movement. So we have the irony of a black woman imitating a white woman who was imitating a black woman – and this black woman had herself been in black-face as a child. Sophie Tucker, who loved the black sound, went on in black-face in the very early days because of the nature of her voice. She was called a 'coon shouter', a term we wince at today. It meant a white performer who sounded like a black performer. ROSETTA REITZ

You notice they said 'shouter' not 'singer'.   BILL DILLARD

But when the Black Swan label, the first black record label, started, they wouldn't take Bessie Smith because her voice was 'too black'. But they took Alberta Hunter and Ethel Waters.   ROSETTA REITZ

White singers, singing like blacks – people like Bing Crosby and Johnny Mercer, Hoagy Carmichael, even Fred Astaire – were probably the first real hipsters, the first to really absorb the essence of what the black singers were doing. In their work from the early thirties, you could hear the black influence on rhythm come creeping into the culture. Then you hear it come out when they are not trying to ape black singers or imitate the accent, but are absorbing it into a style, rather than a black-face, vaudeville thing. These singers use black rhythmic things to express themselves musically, not in order to sound like a black person.   DAVE FRISHBERG

I enjoy hearing Fred Astaire singing a song more than any *real* singer.   CLEO LAINE

Fred Astaire is apparently very, very modest about his singing. But I love it. It is so direct. It's somehow what singing is *about*.   RICHARD RODNEY BENNETT

Fred Astaire has a wonderful way of dealing, with insouciance, with a light touch, with those *down* songs we get stuck with.   MEL TORME

He had a mind. What you're dealing with is a question of the psyche.   BOBBY COLE

He could always *imply* the notes. And he projects a lyric in the most intelligent and musical and sophisticated way. All those composers – Gershwin, Kern, Cole Porter, Irving Berlin – liked the way he did their songs. Someone paid me a high compliment when they said I sounded in some measure like Fred Astaire.   BARBARA CARROLL

My native woodnote and often off-key voice is what I call 'flatsy through the nose'. When I hear my voice on recordings, I get a bit depressed but my phrasing and enunciation is a redeeming factor. HOAGY CARMICHAEL

I was very nervous about meeting Hoagy last year, because he's had a fine life and he's hung out with all the heavy jazz cats in his day and everybody's recorded his songs. But he liked our record and he was very funny and kind to us. He said things like, 'It doesn't matter what you sound like. My songs will make you sound great.' GEORGIE FAME

After 'To Have and Have Not', I was mentioned for every picture in which a world-weary character in bad repair sat around and sang or leaned over a piano. It was usually the part of the hound-dog-faced old musical philosopher noodling on the honky-tonk piano, saying to a tart with a heart of gold: 'He'll be back, honey. He's all man.' HOAGY CARMICHAEL

Bing Crosby could make anything swing. He had the real instinctive jazz rhythm grasp. DAVE FRISHBERG

Bing was born hep. HOAGY CARMICHAEL

Mr Perfect Time, he was always *there*, absolutely. And there's a simplicity about the way he did it. When we were recording or just singing together, Bing and I were always so comfortable. ROSEMARY CLOONEY

For a great many years I was a bit hostile to Bing Crosby, because of what I thought were certain of his political persuasions. As a result, when I was hired to do a Broadway show for a couple of weeks with him, I was prepared to really dislike him. When he arrived at rehearsal, well ahead of time, prepared to go to work, we all sat down. And it was a full orchestra, complete with string section. We began rehearsing his first tune. And this man opened his mouth, and the same dulcet, very mellow, fluid sounds that were reproduced on records, these same sounds I heard sitting up at the back of the orchestra. And I thought, does he have a neck micro-phone? Because I wasn't prepared to deal with the *sound* of this person. And he didn't. And he wasn't shouting, he was just singing. GRADY TATE

★

What happened to all those women? Well, the economy has every-thing to do with the kind of music we get, and the Depression changed a lot. In the roaring twenties, people were going out, out, out, spending money, dancing madness. In the Depression, people couldn't go out – it was 'I'm home about eight, just me and the radio.' So the radio changed the sound of American music. ROSETTA REITZ

And in the thirties the amplified systems began to come in. That was a lifesaver for lots of them. BILL DILLARD

The radio discriminated against the black voices. So that's when you got Connee Boswell, who really was a black voice in a white woman.

And Mildred Bailey was the same thing. That's why they were so popular. And great. It was a very big thing in this country – a white woman with a black sound.   ROSETTA REITZ

We did a gig with a jazz band and one of the boys said, 'Listen to this album.' It was the Boswell Sisters, and it was all so far away in time and style, it seemed like new to us. We did a couple of their things, like 'Heebie Jeebies', styling it as closely as possible to the record, and it took hours of work. We were intrigued because it was actually a vocal blend rather than lead vocalist and two backing singers, which is usual now. And the blend was so tight that we took a long time to pick out some of the parts when we came to work on it.   SWEET SUBSTITUTE

It will take a bit of explaining to tell you just how the Boswells did their thing in those days, because we got arguments from all sides, but I'm happy to say that we won. Not, however, without much sweat, tears and sometimes almost blood. Our trio arrangements were never read from paper, although we were all musicians and could darn well read music upside down and backwards. We lil old Boswell gals knew *best* what was best for us. We revolutionized not only the style of singing, the beat, the placing of voices, the way-out harmony, but also the musical world in general.   CONNEE BOSWELL

They all played musical instruments. They started off in a church choir, deep South. Connee Boswell was in a wheelchair – she'd wear a huge great ball-gown and they'd wheel her on. When they did radio sessions, they'd muffle the piano with a blanket, and get their heads very close together. And the three voices would be the three front-line instruments. You knew right away it was them.   SWEET SUBSTITUTE

I talk about all these ladies in my show. And I say one singer they always overlook is Mildred Bailey. She was a jazz woman through and through.   CARRIE SMITH

I never saw Mildred or Lee Wiley but I have albums of both of them and I think they're fantastic. They both seemed to have something that musicians liked. They had deep feelings and their emotions came through a song. That's what jazz musicians like. And their sound, also. And their rhythmic thing, too. Musicians like that. CHRIS CONNOR

Mildred Bailey happens to be one of the best girl singers that ever *lived*. In my book she's either number one or two. I'd put Ella, then probably Mildred and then Billie. Mildred didn't have the ability to improvise like Ella, no, she didn't. But what a beat. And what a sense of phrasing. And intelligence. And shading. Dynamics. Marvellous taste in accompanists – she used Teddy Wilson and all the good guys. Great taste. Mildred *knew*. She was uncompromising as far as jazz was concerned. As far as people were concerned, too.   PETER DEAN

Mildred and Billie were my two. I was their go-fer. Mildred used to call me her little sister. Because I was a little fat kid, she'd tell everybody we were related.   SYLVIA SYMS

She was a tough chick, and foul-mouthed. That woman had a foul mouth. And she married a great man, Red Norvo, as you know.
PETER DEAN

A strange combo, we used to call it, but it lasted a long time.
HOAGY CARMICHAEL

She chose what she wanted, how she wanted to do it, and did it her way. Totally involved with jazz.   BARBARA CARROLL

Mildred was very vain. And a compulsive eater, I would think. Oh yes, she was quite fiery. And she had a great zest for life. Liked, I think, most earthly pleasures. She liked her dogs. And she liked her husband. And she did not have that one weakness so many female singers seem to have. Unlike many singers, you never heard about Mildred Bailey being under the finger of a man. She believed in herself. And she had a lot to believe in. Like most professionals, she didn't talk about what she did, she went out and did it. She always worked with good jazz musicians, always. And she could swing, God, yes. Marvellous diction. And a wicked sense of humour, just wicked. But she had a good time. Loved to laugh.   BOBBY SHORT

Mildred was a victim of the culture. She didn't have the popular career she should have had because of her weight problems. And you know Dinah Washington died because of the diet pills . . . victims.   ROSETTA REITZ

Lee Wiley, yes. Love to listen to her. She sure had something individual.   JIMMY ROWLES

I like the coolness in the way Lee Wiley approached a song. It sounded like she was a very sophisticated person, but I understand she was a down-home kind of lady.   DAVE FRISHBERG

You don't know much about Lee Wiley because, actually, I suppose she didn't do that much, or make that many records. She was only around in certain areas. I don't think she performed that much, either. She was a musicians' singer, a special cult singer, who had a wonderful husky, throaty sound, a very intriguing sound. BARBARA CARROLL

I think musicians liked her because her rhythmic concept was very nice and fluid and easy. And, for her time, like it or not, she was sexual, which a lot of people thought was an important aspect of what girl singers did. Let's just say the forties gentlemen found Lee Wiley a sexual kind of singer.   DIGBY FAIRWEATHER

She had good taste, too. The mood was always there and the lovely sound she made, always. By the time I got to meet her, any professional career she'd had was over; she didn't care about singing. She never really had to do it for a living. In her earlier career she recorded, she had a radio show, and that's really as far as it went. I heard about her when I was in my teens, and she was a legend, you know. I met her, I guess, about ten years later, here in New York. And she was charming and easy and sweet. And she would sing in my house or your house, but she had no desire to get out and sing. She told me one day, 'You know, it's one thing if you've got a job and you *have* to go out and sing. But if I'm going to sing just for one night, I've got to buy a dress and get my hair done and have this and have that, and then rehearse some numbers.' And she said, 'I just don't care to go through all that again.' And she didn't.   BOBBY SHORT

I don't know why Ethel Waters' name doesn't come up more often. Her phrasing and her musical ability was incredible. It was *intelligent* phrasing. Not many singers have that. I suppose it was to do with her acting ability.   HELEN MERRILL

And I used to love Irene Kral. She never got to be where she should have.   JIMMY ROWLES

Irene was Roy's sister, so she was sort of born to the music life. She'd always say, 'Got any new songs?' So I always gave her my lead sheets. And I think she's recorded more of my songs than any one singer. She was very good but I guess she was never really fulfilled as a singer.   BOB DOROUGH

She was very respectful of the songs she sang, very accurate. I'm pleased with her versions of my songs. It's a little deadpan, a little

austere, maybe, but I'd rather have that than the over-emotional.
DAVE FRISHBERG

I loved her. She had such a good sound and assurance. And she did things *with* a note, rather than altering a note, that were wonderful.   CHARLES COCHRAN

She studied how to make the sound and how you handle it. And she would warm up every day, sit in front of the piano and do the scales.   ROY KRAL

She did her last album when she was staying with us and she was dying of cancer, and she knew she was going to die.   JACKIE CAIN

I'm writing a song in her memory.   BOB DOROUGH

★

I run into an awful lot of girls who came up singing with the big bands.   ROSEMARY CLOONEY

Travelling with a big band is like being an inmate in a travelling zoo.   HOAGY CARMICHAEL

The big bands were the popular music of the *world*, at one point. It was a very exciting time. It enabled you to be what we would term today a superstar.   WOODY HERMAN

All the great bands played at the Savoy Ballroom – a unique place at the time. Well, they say the joint was jumping. Those words were literally an actuality. Because if you approached the place, you could see the windows *moving*, big bay windows, vibrating with the beat of the music. As you walked in, you could feel the place *vibrating*, the floors, the walls, the windows, everything.   DUKE JORDAN

Those bands were extremely demanding – the life, and the music.
ROSETTA REITZ

The bands were very polished. And the singers didn't do very much experimenting.   CHET BAKER

Yes, I suppose it was mostly jazz by association for the band singers. But, I mean, at seventeen, what can you have a feeling *for*? You've not had too much experience, really. Anita O'Day was probably the exception.   ROSEMARY CLOONEY

Anita is just fantastic now. Better than ever. I saw her earlier this year.   CHRIS CONNOR

Singers like Anita O'Day can be absolutely overwhelming. I saw her recently and it's like I'd never seen her before. She was so good and so surprising.   RICHARD RODNEY BENNETT

Anita was the ultimate hip chick. And she was such a facile singer, her intuition was so good all the time. I couldn't get enough of it. Not long ago I went to hear her, and I was saying all these things to someone at the table. And she stopped singing and said, '*When* Miss Clooney stops talking, I'll continue.' And I felt so awful. And she never gave me the chance to explain.   ROSEMARY CLOONEY

She's a self-made voice. And she's an inspiration to me. But she won't talk about it or how she does it, that's her secret. The only advice she ever gave me as a friend was, 'Don't focus so much on the story. Don't sing the melody line.' She always wanted me to get more into the improvisational way of singing. She wanted me to doctor every line as a horn player would do.   CHARLES COCHRAN

Anita is to me much more of a jazz singer than I am, because she does a lot of scatting and the instrumental things that a horn does. I know she listens to instrumentalists and gets very influenced by musicians' phrasings, the saxophone lines and things like that. CHRIS CONNOR

Anita never listens to singers.   CHARLES COCHRAN

When I was about seventeen, I listened to all of them, Ella, Mildred, Billie. Then I went to a movie and saw Martha Raye do 'Mr Paganini', and I thought, that's the way to do it. And then I started following musicians. I used to follow Buddy de Franco and copy his licks.   ANITA O'DAY

She's a jazz person through and through. She's even a jazz *cook*. CHARLES COCHRAN

Martha Raye is one of the best singers that ever lived. And she is an inspiration today, for me, every night that we work together. And she really is like a child, because she doesn't believe me when I tell her.   ROSEMARY CLOONEY

I've heard Anita say her favourite singer is Martha Raye. And it would figure, because Martha Raye has a cool jazz, no-vibrato sound, verging on flat, in that very groovy way, on certain notes. CHARLES COCHRAN

I remember seeing June Christy, when my sister and I were with

Tony Pastor's band. She was, of course, with Kenton. She fitted so well with the band's sound and it must have been intensely hard work. We would get back – we stayed at the same place – and we'd lean out of the window until she came home, just to say goodnight to her. To me she was the California look and the California kind of singer. She meant lovely spring dresses and the suntan and the blonde, blonde hair. ROSEMARY CLOONEY

The California school was like the atmosphere out there, which is very laid back. You never let too much emotion show in your playing, it wasn't the hip thing to do. Even a singer who came out of California tended to have a very special sound, a lot more *dead* tone, the vibrato very much controlled. CHET BAKER

It was an extraordinary vocal quality she had, and it sure sums up the period, an emotional quality. She always liked good songs. And, of course, I liked June personally, everyone did. JIMMY LYON

And then for Stan to find someone like Chris Connor afterward, isn't it amazing? They were all like children of each other from Anita down. That sound they all had was very affecting in a way, I know. Very intense, not exactly in tune, no vibrato really.
ROSEMARY CLOONEY

Anita, June and I all sang with the Kenton band and they called us a school. Well it's pretty good company, let me tell you. But if you listen to our records, you'll hear the differences. CHRIS CONNOR

Kay Starr, I think, had more experience with bands than any of us. Katie worked with Joe Venuti, Charlie Barnet and a lot of very, very good musicians. She can do so many different kinds of things. She's wonderful looking, and she's got that wonderful, rich voice that is just *barrelhouse*, it's so full. She always was a *swinger*, oh boy. She can just rock the house *out*. ROSEMARY CLOONEY

Kay can *shout*. But she got moved into that commercial thing. They made that choice. Like Dinah Shore, she was very jazz orientated at first. PETER DEAN

There was the style of the decorative band singer of the forties, the Doris Day type, that became part of the mode. I don't hold it against them that they had their eyes on Hollywood and all that. They move where the money is. ROSETTA REITZ

In 1931 we were booked to play the Oriental Theater in Chicago for the first time. The producer thought it would enhance our show if we were to add a girl singer. Although Ivie Anderson was not well known at the time, I soon found that she was really an extraordinary artist and an extraordinary person as well. She had great dignity, and she was greatly admired by everybody everywhere we went, at home and abroad. She became one of our mainstays and highlights, and she gave some unforgettable performances. She stopped the show cold at the Palladium in London in 1933. Her routine normally consisted of four songs, but while she was singing 'Stormy Weather' the audience and all the management brass broke down crying and applauding. The brass came backstage to say, 'Don't let her sing anything but "Stormy Weather".' Even she couldn't follow that. They still talk about Ivie, and every girl singer we've had since has had to try to prevail over the Ivie Anderson image.   DUKE ELLINGTON

Ivie Anderson was lovely. Not showy. She was very neat and smart looking. Wore her hair plain. She was a very plain sort of person. She was the best of Duke's singers. She was with him for a long time and he never really did replace her. She retired to go back home and she died a long time ago.   ADELAIDE HALL

Betty Roche was a unique singer.   DUKE ELLINGTON

She had a pretty good repertoire but just about the only thing she ever recorded with Duke was 'Take the "A" Train'. She was a lovely person, and she's had a tragic life. She became very ill and she's in a wheelchair. There's a lot of interest in Duke Ellington now and I'm sure she could sing, even like that. But it seems she's lost heart. There's no reason why she shouldn't sing. A good friend of mine and of hers has tried to pull her out to do some concerts, and she just won't go.   JULIA STEELE

I often wondered how Ella and Helen Humes and the singers with the bands could *do* the one-night stand thing, year after year. I did it once with Benny Carter and when I got back to New York, I kissed the *ground*.   MAXINE SULLIVAN

Ella, I don't even call the First Lady of Song. She is the High Priestess of Song.   MEL TORME

Ella is one of the champs.   MILT GABLER

Ella was the queen. In the beginning she sang with all that freedom and all that excitement. I was at school and I started a club that went to the Savoy Ballroom every Friday night. I was a kind of ringleader. And I became friends with most of the bandleaders there. One night, Chick Webb comes over and says, 'Hey Peter, I want you to meet a little girl. And I want you to hear this girl sing.' And he trotted out Ella Fitzgerald and we went *nuts* for her. We all loved her. And the piano player in my high school band changed his name to Van Alexander and wrote 'A Tisket, A Tasket', which was a worldwide hit for her. Isn't that cute?   PETER DEAN

Chick Webb was very protective of Ella, who was just about a contemporary of Billie Holiday. And Norman Granz later on was very protective. Maybe, like so many singers, her love-life was kind of disappointing, but her work hasn't been ruined, like Billie's was.   ROSETTA REITZ

Her ears are perfect. She's born with it. She was born with that talent and then she developed it, by osmosis.   HELEN MERRILL

Jimmy Jones used to call her 'Perfect pitch bitch'.   MARILYN MOORE

I know I play different chords and things with her, different from her other pianists. Whenever I do something, she'll jump right on it – it gives her ideas. That's what she likes from her accompanists. JIMMY ROWLES

I guess when I started I may have tried to sound like Ella, because she was the newest thing on the scene.   MAXINE SULLIVAN

Every tour I've ever made with her convinced me that singing is her whole life. I remember once in Genoa, Italy, we sat down to eat and the restaurant was empty except for Lester Young and his wife and Ella and me. So while we waited to give our breakfast order, I pulled out my guitar and she and Lester started making up fabulous things on the blues. Another time, when we were touring Switzerland, instead of gossiping with the rest of the troupe on the bus, she and I would get together and she'd take some tune like 'Blue Lou' and sing it every way in the world. She would try to exhaust every possibility, as if she were trying to develop improvisation to a new point by ad-libbing lyrically too, the way calypso singers do.   BARNEY KESSEL

Most of the singers who work at all are copying Ella, Billie or Sarah.   SHEILA JORDAN

I know I've taken from three singers. But I haven't done what a lot of girls did, that is, take their obvious surface things, that people can immediately recognize. With Ella, I knew I had to work on ideas. With Sarah, I knew I could never achieve that *sound*, but at least with what I've got, I tried to make my voice sound as good, as round. From Billie, it was what she got from words.   CLEO LAINE

I don't think it was until Ella Fitzgerald that a singer became the headliner over the band. Chick Webb realized what a treasure he had found and built things round her. Prior to that the band had been the main attraction. Even when we did vaudeville, we would have a singer, but the band was the headliner.   BILL DILLARD

I always did say that the Swing Era never swung itself out. But the war came. And the bands had to break up. And there were a lot of small combos on the road.   MAXINE SULLIVAN

Louis Jordan had a marvellous small group with him, wonderful songs, wonderful presentation. He didn't have a *voice*, but he could sell a song.   JOE LEE WILSON

I never met Louis Jordan but I used to *love* his work. You know, Georgie Fame does 'Let the Good Times Roll', but I used to do it before he was *born*. And at the time it was daring modern music.
RAY ELLINGTON

★

I think the people I admire most, like Sarah Vaughan, Carmen McRae, Mark Murphy, Shirley Horn, come out of being piano players.   RICHARD RODNEY BENNETT

Sarah, she's my baby. I always thought of myself as trying to be a musician-singer – to sing music. Sarah does the same thing, I guess. That's why I was so impressed when I first heard her. And I got her with us. Because it was the first time I heard a singer who wanted to do the same thing, who would take a chord and improvise and sing the changes like a trumpet player or a saxophone player.   BILLY ECKSTINE

She has the background as a musician and as a jazz person. And that voice – the quality of a *saint*.   BOBBY TUCKER

It's hardly possible, but after twenty-five or thirty years in this business, Sarah is twice or three times as great as ever. I heard her at Carnegie Hall. And it was really an incredible evening of enjoyment. Something unplanned, impromptu, can turn out to be

magnificent, because of the creative quality of that kind of music.
MILT JACKSON

Sarah Vaughan improvises. Sarah Vaughan will sing, say 'Lush Life' differently every night. Sarah is the most spontaneous and creative singer I've ever had the pleasure of working with. And I've worked with the best singers in the world.   GRADY TATE

She can play some beautiful stuff on piano. She can sight read. Give her a piece of music, she can sing it. I think Sarah is a real musician. Ella is a natural musician. Carmen is a musician. Peggy Lee is a musician. Frank Sinatra, Vic Damone, Tony Bennett, all nice musicians. They all have their different levels of musical knowledge, of course. I'll give you an example. With Sarah, you can play *anything* behind her. You can make a fight of it. She hears everything. She can go in any direction.   JIMMY ROWLES

I'll be glad when people find out that I do not know everything. I know everything I know. Hey, that's a good line.   SARAH VAUGHAN

And there's an awful lot to admire in Mel Torme – he's equipped.
BOBBY COLE

Of course, Mel's a bitch. I love Mel.   BILLY ECKSTINE

He's the Buddy Rich of the voice, to me. I'm left dazed and dazzled and impressed.   DAVE FRISHBERG

Mel Torme thinks he's the only white man singing jazz.   BETTY CARTER

A lot of the great singers are good pianists, even if they don't accompany themselves all the time.   PAT SMYTHE

I've heard Carmen McRae get up in a club and just accompany herself and it was marvellous.   RICHARD RODNEY BENNETT

That's when Carmen *sings*. When she steps to the piano and begins to sing, she turns into someone else. I think it's because when she's at the piano she's got her hands to worry about – this is all unconscious, of course – and what's left is what we get as the singer, the real, true, sweet, musical person that's singing to us.   DAVE FRISHBERG

Carmen can be difficult. She can be tough. She's OK though. I like to fight with her. I love to fight with her, she can *fight*.   JIMMY ROWLES

You've got to catch her in a moment when she steps out of that tough lady thing. She doesn't sing soft much any more. But I know the problem with that. Sometimes your voice gets to a point when it only works at a loud volume. The voice that works most nights is the one that's louder.   MARK MURPHY

★

If you're working in joints, sometimes it looks like a joint. Sometimes it looks like a real swell place, and you didn't know it's a joint. But it's a *joint*.   ABBEY LINCOLN

Once a saloon singer, always a saloon singer, as Bobby Short says.   MAXINE SULLIVAN

I can tell you, singing in bars almost drove *me* to drink.   MARK MURPHY

When I started the audiences in clubs were mostly drunks. They used to come to nightclubs to get drunk. It was disgusting, and it ran me out of the business for a while.   HELEN MERRILL

When clubs are great, they're really great. There's no atmosphere like a club atmosphere. But they're hard, hard on the voice. There's a lot of smoke and sometimes you have to do three shows a night. You have to deal with drunks, people talking, unresponsive audiences for no particular reason. It's draining when you give a lot and you don't get anything back.   SUSANNAH McCORKLE

What I hate is getting home and everything smells of smoke, your hair, your clothes, your music, everything.   SHEILA JORDAN

One feels so unfresh.   BOBBY SHORT

Listen, I was working table to table in this little place in Pittsburgh, 1936, without a microphone. That's why you went from table to table. Sure, you had to invent. You keep singing the song over and over until they spring – that's the word for giving you a tip. I didn't have too much, you know, *personality*, so I only came back with nickels and dimes. Some of the girls could take the money off the table between their legs, if they were built that way. But the first time I pulled my dress up, the manager said, 'Maxine, you keep your dress *down*.'   MAXINE SULLIVAN

I was still at school and I suddenly discovered a place called W. 52nd

Street. I found out from some friends that if I got on the subway where I lived in Brooklyn, I could get down to 49th Street for a nickel and walk. Which I did. Scared out of my bird, let me tell you. I didn't know what I was going to find. I'd spent the whole day trying to beat my folks for a dime to get there. Then I waited till they went to bed, and I sneaked out the window.   SYLVIA SYMS

52nd Street in those days was just alive with musicians and performers. So I ended up where *everybody* could hear me sing. Not only was I lucky to get into the Onyx Club, first try, but there were a million singers who must have wondered, 'How did *she* get in there', and didn't make it.   MAXINE SULLIVAN

It was summer time and I went past club after club. And there was no air-conditioning, so the doors were all open. And I could hear everything on the street, because I didn't have but a nickel to get home with. Every other door was a club. And in each of these clubs there was somebody wonderful. And I stopped and listened. And when a set was over I'd move down. And then I came to a club and Billie Holiday was working there. And that's when I came to know what I really wanted to do. She became my tutor, my mentor, my idol. She was everything to me.   SYLVIA SYMS

People are very romantic about 52nd Street, but it was terrible really. For a headliner musician, the scale was eighty-eight dollars a week. And if you weren't the top, which meant you started later and worked later, number two scale was sixty-six dollars a week. Which was hardly adequate to live on, even then.   BOBBY TUCKER

Jazz was the only good thing on 52nd Street.   MILT JACKSON

It seemed like music was just bursting out of the doors, everywhere. It was just like one big party. And after work, we'd take the train or the bus up to Harlem, because most of us lived in Harlem, and walk through the streets at two or three in the morning – goodness, you couldn't do that in the *daytime* now. And we'd go on to one of the little places where the music would go on all night, and have so much *fun*. I managed to get to New York in time to have a good time in Harlem. So many of the famous places and the little places have gone, it makes you sad to see Harlem now.   ROSE MURPHY

It was quite safe, then, you could go anywhere. Harlem was the centre of theatrical entertainment at that time. We just didn't have the violence, the muggings, and the narcotics situation, all the dangers that are around the streets today.   BILL DILLARD

52nd Street is all high-rise buildings, office blocks now. MILT JACKSON

It was 52nd Street and the war. It was a day and night thing, every moment was a swinging thing. There *was* no day or night. Then suddenly it all went. ANITA O'DAY

Everybody was crazy about Mabel Mercer. Billie Holiday used to come off after her show, go freshen up and say, 'Let's go to hear Mabel.' And we'd go right across to Tony's. MILT GABLER

Her scene was the product of that thirties elegance thing, you know. She made her name in Paris at Bricktop's, and she says one night the Duchess of Windsor came in, and urged them both to leave Paris because the Nazis were at the door. So Mabel came to New York. And she rather quickly started gathering a little family, and her fans are just so loyal and most of them are rich. And they supported her beautifully all these years. MARK MURPHY

Mabel, now, she's nothing to do with the swinging tradition or improvisation. And yet, you know, Lady got more songs from Mabel Mercer than anybody else. BOBBY TUCKER

When singers like Frank Sinatra say, 'Mabel Mercer taught me everything about singing a song', they're talking about phrasing. They're not talking about the sound or the harmonic ideas or anything like that. They're talking about how she delivers a lyric. JIMMY LYON

She makes you feel you've never heard the lyric before. RICHARD RODNEY BENNETT

I was working with Peggy Lee and as soon as I finished, I used to love to race to that place, and go up there, sit down in a corner and just listen to Mabel. I used to go there every night. I always liked her best in a room where lights were low. That was her – what's the word – milieu? You could hear a pin drop. I don't know how she did it. No, no microphone, she didn't need it. It was her delivery I loved. Just to sit and listen to her doing all those way-out songs she knows, and she knows so many. And she always looked so *elegant*, the way she sat there on her stool in that little pin spot. People just fell in love with her the moment they saw her. JIMMY ROWLES

That kind of intimate singing is hard to do. JIMMY LYON

Now, Blossom Dearie is doing a great job in finding new songs and

54

rediscovering old ones. And then hundreds of singers take them up.   PAT SMYTHE

You've *got* to listen to Blossom. If you don't, you lost the whole thing. She needs your absolute attention, you know.   SHIRLEY HORN

The *song* really shines when Blossom sings it. As opposed to Blossom shining. She shines, too, of course, but the song comes across.   DAVE FRISHBERG

I still find piano bars a bit scary because you're so close to the people. It's not so scary in a big auditorium, because you're singing into the dark.   RICHARD RODNEY BENNETT

I think this piano bar thing goes back to the movies, 'Casablanca' you know. And so, if you've got a black piano player who sings, they think it's even better.   MIKE McKENZIE

I'm a concert animal now, not so much a cabaret animal. I found that with the smoking and the atmosphere and the late, late hours, I was losing my voice. And I like to sing.   CLEO LAINE

But there's something in a club situation that you don't get on a concert stage. In a club you get more chances to sing in a night. Whereas, in a concert, you're out there, and then it's over in an hour, or whatever. And you think, oh God, I was just getting warmed up. And you're less apt to try ultra-creative things on a concert, you're more apt to take those chances in a club.   SHEILA JORDAN

The jazz format is loose. I prefer to hear jazz people in a club rather than at Carnegie Hall. They perform more comfortably.   HELEN MERRILL

I do mostly concerts now, so you get a more interested audience. You know they've come to hear *you*.   NORMA WINSTONE

Any place that is not a music room or a concert hall has the disadvantage that people will be talking. Utopia is a concert situation, because there are no distractions, no smoking, no drinking, no talking, no moving around. But there is a kind of intimacy, a certain kind of informality and rapport you can achieve in a room like the one I work in now. It's not like work at all.   BARBARA CARROLL

But the best way is not to be on stage at all, but right in the middle.

Or in an arena type of situation, when the people are around you. I don't like to stand in front of the musicians so working in the round is great for me. I learned this from my dance experience. The audience can pick up the total vibrations all around you – they're not separated, with you at the back and them in the front.   JEANNE LEE

Churches do fabulous things for the voice.   NORMA WINSTONE

I was involved in church music for about ten years. All new jazz works, by the way. Getting the message across was a total contact with the audience.   SHEILA JORDAN

Being a singer really means being part of the community. It does not mean just making a record and singing in clubs and concerts. It means going to the children, working with them, working in factories, community centres, old people's homes, with people of all ages. And it means working from the jazz aesthetic, from improvisation in the multi-media arts.   JEANNE LEE

I was always seeking to be part of the group rather than a stand-up singer. So I would not stand up front. I didn't even want to be introduced, because there's so much attention on the singer. I've also had this idea of doing concerts in the dark. Because you become freer when you don't have to have this *image*. And people can hear better.   JAY CLAYTON

It's difficult because there are so few places and so few choices to make as to where you *can* sing.   MARILYN MOORE

I've played the worst places: no kind of lighting or sound systems. And I've been singing for thirty years. *And I still play them.*   CHRIS CONNOR

I came out of the business for a while in 1957 because my music had gone out of style.   MAXINE SULLIVAN

You get into the cruelty of style change. Like, when Bessie Smith couldn't get a job at the beginning of the thirties, because fashions had changed. Then, in the early forties the style changed again, and Sarah Vaughan appeared and she became Queen, and Billie Holiday became a sort of collector's item. I'm treating my chops like gold, you know, to make sure I can work through this era, because you never know how long it's going to last.   MARK MURPHY

They're talking about tearing Carnegie Hall down. Like the Savoy

Ballroom in Harlem, they tore that down. We're always tearing down our history. The Apollo Theater is still there, who knows how long for. Everyone worked there – Bessie, Billie, everybody. It'll be torn down, because it doesn't mean anything to them. And this rubs off on the music, too. Just another throwaway thing.   CARRIE SMITH

They don't believe in excellence in this country, they believe in the *latest*. Overnight sensations.   LEON THOMAS

3
How?

. . . they talk about their apprenticeships . . .

All I know was that music was something I had to do till I died.
SHEILA JORDAN

Singing is a thing you're compelled to do. And you can't help
yourself. You look at the musicians, and you think, God, it will be
fun to sing with them. And, in your mind you are already singing
with them. You feel yourself doing this thing, you hear yourself.
You do it before you do it.   JOE WILLIAMS

I don't think I ever decided to do it for life – I think *it*
decided.   MOSE ALLISON

Probably some ancestral promptings made me want to do it.   LEON
THOMAS

I feel driven. I feel I've *got* to find a way to keep singing, because I
love it so much.   SUSANNAH McCORKLE

You'll probably find that our backgrounds are boringly similar – the
need to do it. People can have all the instincts for music and still
never get on stage. But the fact that you *have* to get out and put it
out in front of the world already tells a story, I think. Any kind of
public performance is a *need*.   HELEN MERRILL

There's a certain feeling you get – oh, there's no feeling in the world
like it, when it's really *happening*.   SHEILA JORDAN

The needful background forces you to want the applause and attention. But many singers are very shy. And the shrinking, the shyness, is another sign of the needful background. Sometimes acceptance helps you to get over that, if you can believe it.   HELEN MERRILL

When I went on stage and sang 'It's De-Lovely' or 'Organ Grinder's Swing', I got the love I craved. I didn't need anyone. For me, music equalled love.   ANITA O'DAY

It only occurs to me now, when I look back, how determined I was. I wouldn't have done anything if I had not been determined. I knew I wanted to do it. And I knew it was difficult.   NORMA WINSTONE

I purposely kept myself hungry. I didn't get any other kind of job. I said, 'I'm going to live from singing, because that's the only way I'll have the nerve to go out and do what I have to do to serve my apprenticeship.'   SUSANNAH McCORKLE

But, if you love it enough, you know you have to go on with all this. Whatever stage you are at, you need to find people who like what you do. Because people can be very cold. People can kill you stone dead.   JAY CLAYTON

There's a lot of rejection, too, in a singer's life. And what causes us to *continue* is a whole other story.   HELEN MERRILL

When I started singing it was hard. But not as hard as it is now.
SALENA JONES

I have no idea how one would begin to get started today. Because when I came along, you would be recommended by somebody. People would say, 'Hey, get Joe for this job.'   JOE WILLIAMS

People say, 'Where have you worked?' And if you haven't worked anywhere, 'Get some experience working somewhere.' It's the Catch 22 situation, isn't it?   MARIAN MONTGOMERY

When I was starting out, groups used to ring you up and say, 'Do you want a gig?' You went along with your standards, and you did a gig.   PEPI LEMER

These days, singers have to make their own gigs. They have to be leaders right away. That's hard. It's better to be a singer with a band first, let someone else be in charge.   JAY CLAYTON

I was working during the day, but I started doing awful gigs and weddings and things. You'd just go along and say to the bandleader,

'Well, what do you want me to do?' And he'd say, 'You sing a song when I point to you.' And you'd just sing the song through once, then they'd play up to the middle, and you'd come in again and take it out. But at the time, I started making up my own bits, you see. In the middle, instead of singing the tune, I'd sing something else. I was sort of driven to do it. And I started getting comments, 'Where did you get that from? What record did you get that off?' And I'd say, 'I made it up.' And it didn't go down very well.   NORMA WINSTONE

I had no idea that I might have any talent which might enable me to make a living from jazz. But I managed to work myself into day jobs which had something to do with the music – instrument firms, record companies. Then I got a letter from Maxime Saury, a French clarinet player I'd taken under my wing when he was in London, offering me two months' work at the Vieux Colombier in Paris. So that was my first full-time professional job, and the date I take my singing career from. I was able to say, 'I'm a singer', though I had to go back to secretarial work a few times until singing jobs became more frequent than typing jobs.   BERYL BRYDEN

Joe Glaser told me about a friend of his, who had a girl who worked in the washroom of his club. They couldn't keep her in the washroom, because she was always trying to sing with the band . . . They took me down there and told this girl, 'Now, I want you to sing for this orchestra leader.' She sang a couple of blues numbers and sounded good, so I said, 'I'm playing at the Regal Theater. Come on out and sing with me tomorrow' . . . She got up and sang 'Evil Gal Blues' and, boy, she broke it up. Her real name was Ruth Jones, but I asked her if she would mind if I changed it. 'I don't care what you call me, so long as you give me the job.' 'Okay, you're hired. From now on you're Dinah Washington.'   LIONEL HAMPTON

This is how you do it, my dear. You get to know musicians. You're in the places where they are. And then you ask them if you can sing a song. Be very charming, not *too* pushy. And be prepared. Know your song, know your key. And sing it. And then someone will hear you, and take you out for dinner, and give you a job. And there you are.   ADELAIDE HALL

It's easy. Hustle. Hang out. *Keep* hanging out.   JOE LEE WILSON

There are all different shades of blues. There's all different shades of singer.   BETTY CARTER

I was working in an after-hours place in Pittsburgh where musicians would drop in. And I got a lot of encouragement. And Gladys Mosier, who played with Ina Ray Hutton's band, said, 'If you ever come to New York, look me up.' I saved my money. I was working with a piano player called Jenny Dillard, and I said, 'I'm going to New York.' And she said, 'Come on, let's go.' So we got an overnight excursion one Sunday morning to come back on Monday – I don't know what we expected to do *overnight*. But luckily she had a brother in Harlem, so that's where we first landed. And I called Gladys Mosier. 'Hello.' 'Who's this?' 'It's Maxine.' 'Maxine who?' You know the thing. Anyway, she said, 'You can't go back tomorrow.' So we decided to stay. And she met us on the Wednesday, and we auditioned in every gin mill from 155th Street in Harlem down to 52nd Street, just walked in to the places. Then I got to sing for Carl Kress, who was part owner of the Onyx in 52nd Street. And I went to work there on the Friday.   MAXINE SULLIVAN

One thing about New York, it's always a surprise to you.   JOE LEE WILSON

I came to New York at the tail-end of the 52nd Street era. And I found that if the musicians thought you were a, quote, lady musician, forget it. But if they thought you could *play* then it was all right.   BARBARA CARROLL

When I went to New York it was to play the Famous Door on 52nd Street, opposite Count Basie. But it started when I went to Cleveland to play at a girlfriend's party. And a manager of a club there asked me to play at his place – one little room and a little upright piano.   ROSE MURPHY

I was house singer in a little club in Santa Monica, California. How did I get the job? I just went and sat in. I was confident. It was my first job. Eight bucks a night, four nights a week. It helped, because there were solo artists coming in all the time and I got known. Then there was Bop City, San Francisco, where I met the New York musicians, who were a different kind of player, to be sure. They said, 'Come to New York.' I ended up in New York and thought I'd turn it upside down overnight. Twenty years later, I'm still trying. JOE LEE WILSON

A lot of people come to New York. And a lot of people have been living in New York all their lives. And I come on the excursion with a bar of soap in my bag. And I hit the jackpot.   MAXINE SULLIVAN

I sang in the church when I was eight years old. As long as I can remember, I was singing. I always had the voice. My mother gave me the voice.   BILLY ECKSTINE

The church music was something that everybody could *do*. Whether you could, like, *sing* or not, you could do it. It was something everybody did.   'CLEANHEAD' VINSON

I became one of the lead singers in the choir. I had no professional training, but I learned to sing parts from my church minister. And I did my first concert in 1961, singing gospel music and spirituals at Town Hall, New York, and got some good reviews.   CARRIE SMITH

I didn't have any lessons – we couldn't afford that – but I did music all the time. I just listened. I still do.   HELEN MERRILL

I started singing without music. I would just sing in somebody else's key, somebody else's songs, somebody else's style. I used to sound like Sarah Vaughan when I started. And Ella. And Dinah. I copied them song for song. These people do songs that you like and you learn the song off the record. I had a voice and I hadn't found myself. I was a clone.   SALENA JONES

I was twenty-three when I found I was a singer. I mean I was working as a singer. But it was unintended.   JEANNE LEE

I won the Amateur Hour at the Apollo Theater. The encouragement came when I hit my first two notes, and everybody went quiet. And I thought, aaaaaaaaah.   SALENA JONES

When I told my family I wanted to be a singer, my father said, 'A singer? Everybody can sing.'   JOE LEE WILSON

I must say my father didn't believe that my following music would be of any good to my life. Or to him. I said, 'I'm going to quit law. I want to play piano.' He just went crazy.   ROY KRAL

I had a voice, but my parents were very averse to my having anything to do with being a singer. My father and mother thought that nice children from decent families didn't go into show business. And they did everything they could to dissuade me. And did everything they could to discourage me. And they gave me no help whatsoever. And it took a long time.   SYLVIA SYMS

I wish I had been in an area more conducive to going into the arts, but in the South, anything to do with the arts and emotions was immediately suspect. One was supposed to tread carefully. I never did. Therefore I was disowned by my parents. By my father, literally. I had to laugh and say, 'Exactly what are you disowning me *from*?' MARIAN MONTGOMERY

My mother and father didn't understand jazz, but they knew it was something I wanted to do. Even when friends would say, 'How can you let her go and work with those crazy dope-smoking jazz musicians?' BARBARA CARROLL

My father was a professor of music. But they didn't want me to go into show business at all. But I was picked right out of the chorus to star with Bill Robinson, the great Bojangles. I was known as a very good tap dancer right from the beginning – a natural born gift – you invented your own steps, your own routine, and you'd just go to town. And there you are. ADELAIDE HALL

My father and mother are both singers, so I grew up around their teaching. I made a lot of my *sounds* unconsciously, when I was a kid. BOBBY McFERRIN

I was aware from the earliest age that I could make music. We always had music in the house. My father was a singer – European classical and Afro-American classical music. JEANNE LEE

I had music in school, and when I went to college, someone said 'Why don't you do the music course?' I was studying classical voice, but I actually began to *sing* on weekends. There were two jazz musicians there who turned me on to Coltrane and Mingus. Jazz brought out possibilities I didn't know about. JAY CLAYTON

I've been singing professionally since I was four. I earned my first dollar, in fact, my first fifteen dollars, at the age of four, on Monday nights at the Black Rock restaurant in Chicago. Once I started, I was never out of the business. MEL TORME

I was working at seven, eight years old, showing off. And when I was eleven and a half, I actually went into serious, professional show business. I imagined myself as a bandleader. Well, it seemed very glamorous. Then it all became Duke Ellington, because I thought he was the most elegant. BOBBY SHORT

It was taken for granted that I was going into show business, because of my family. There were five of us kids, all in the business before we could walk. Because one way of getting a round of applause was to bring out the new baby. When I was four, I was sent to live with my aunt, Ella Logan, in Hollywood. She was very into jazz, very ahead of her time. She gave me an Ella record when I was six – not bad exposure, is it? I was performing when I was six – I've got a copy of my MGM contract. Well, I was a show-off and I loved nothing better than being brought down in my nightgown to sing for people at parties.   ANNIE ROSS

I sang since I was three. I was always in time and I was always in tune.   ROSEMARY CLOONEY

I'm seventy-three, and I didn't sing until I was over sixty. I'd been a manager in the music business, and I had a very successful jingle business for years, and everybody kind of knew me. Before the war, I was a fairly cute kid who could dance and sing a bit. But when I was drafted I gave up all thoughts of being a performer, and I was put in charge of shows for the soldiers. When I came out, I had so many wonderful contacts, I went into management full tilt. Then in 1972, I had George Barnes and Bucky Pizzarelli at the St Regis Hotel, and the manager said, 'These guys are wonderful, but I need a singer.' That's when I put my hand up and shuffled up to the microphone and started. And my latest record kind of took off: *Stereo Magazine* voted it one of the best albums of the year.   PETER DEAN

I heard 'Give Me a Pigfoot' by Bessie Smith. And I had that *frisson*, that sort of shiver, of familiarity. I'd never heard it, but I felt I had heard it, or had been waiting to hear it. I became a singer because I fell in love with Bessie Smith.   GEORGE MELLY

I was living in Paris, working as a translator, when I first heard a Billie Holiday record. And I decided I wanted to try singing. I wrote down the titles of all the songs I knew. And there were more than two hundred.   SUSANNAH McCORKLE

I came from a coal-mining town. And we didn't have a radio, didn't have electricity, even. So the only singers I heard were the mountain people, the coal-miners. They'd get drunk and they'd sing.   SHEILA JORDAN

Any music I have must come from inside me, it didn't come from the environment at all. I was brought up on a dairy farm in Queensland, Australia. The only music we had was in a corrugated-iron hall on Saturday nights. But when I heard the blues, I gravitated to it. All I wanted to do was see the world and sing.   JULIE AMIET

I started playing jazz as a teenager, back in what used to be British Guiana. My father got cross because he wanted me to be a concert pianist. But I was a great Ellington fan, and I loved jazz and started playing it and started making money from playing it. MIKE McKENZIE

I used to sing bossa nova, the popular music of Brazil. And I got turned on to jazz. And I heard a lot and decided to come to New York and check it out at the source of it. And I thought it was magic. And I've stayed. FLORA PURIM

I was learning piano at school. I was at a friend's house, playing her Dave Brubeck records, and I looked at the cover, and it talked about 'improvisation'. And it kind of dawned on me just what I was listening to – somebody *improvising* – and I thought, that's clever. NORMA WINSTONE

I was at school and I didn't know what else I could do. My dad had come over in 1933 or so from Jamaica, to study at Kneller Hall, then he went into bands. So there were always musicians around the house. And Dad was always sorting out his arrangements and trooping off. I sang with his band at weekends: he'd say, 'Now don't say you're my daughter, you're my *sister*.' ELAINE DELMAR

I was one of the first of the Americans drifting about Europe in the sixties, because of the rock phenomenon. You could live on so little in those days and there was work all over. Then things got sparse, and I almost retired. I started all over again in the States in 1972. And got back to England in Jubilee year. Now, all these audiences are so nice to me, because I've stuck to it. MARK MURPHY

I wasn't starting in show business. I never had no idea I'd get into show business. I was going to school, about 1928, it was. I went to Buffalo to visit some friends. And they said, 'Come on, Helen, you've got to come out and sing.' And they took me to the Spider Web, ooh, it was a big club. And Al Sears' band was playing there, and that's when I got my first job. HELEN HUMES

There was this audition for a trad band, when I was fifteen. I went along and that was it. I had the job. I've never had a *proper* job since. CAROL KIDD

A girl I knew in college had a summer job at a local TV place and she dared me to go in there, and sing. I did, and they asked me to come back every week. And that's how I met local musicians and they asked me to work with them. People cotton on to youth. And I suppose I looked like Little Mary Sunshine in those days. MARIAN MONTGOMERY

I was a folk singer when I first came to England. I'd made some pop records: one was a minor hit in Zimbabwe. I'm American, but I never sang in America. I was twenty-six, working in a record shop, and I began to get into big band music, dipping into a bit of Billie Holiday, bit of Frank Sinatra. I started reading a few books, and, before I knew it, it was like going to college. I began to get into vintage music. I enjoyed entertaining, and there was a place for a younger singer, reviving a style that had been buried by fashion. One thing led to another. I found a direction, a perch. JOHNNY M

I started off as a rock 'n' roller, copying Jerry Lee Lewis and Fats Domino, back in Lancashire in 1958, packing them in at the local pub. I'd just left school and was working in a cotton factory. Then four of my mates from the factory went on holiday to the inevitable holiday camp in North Wales. And someone said, 'Go on, get up, do your stuff.' So I sang a couple of tunes in the bar. And there was Rory Blackwell, who was one of Britain's first rock 'n' rollers. He offered me a job with his band. My parents were horrified, but instinct told me I ought to give it a crack. So I became a professional musician. And Rory got the sack four weeks later. We came to London, and, to his credit, he got me a job playing in a pub at weekends, passing the box around, living in a hovel in Islington, wide-eyed in the city. Then I had two years in the Larry Parnes stable of rock 'n' rollers – he gave me a new name. And I could write to Dad, 'It's all cool, I'm playing with all these stars.' The turning-point came when I started getting into rhythm and blues with Billy Fury and the Blue Flames. We got the sack for not playing rock 'n' roll, and I didn't work for a few months. There was nothing to do but lay around the room I was sharing, living off the odd bag of chips and playing records. And I heard Billie Holiday, Mose Allison, Chet Baker singing, King Pleasure, *jazz*. It had all gone straight over my head before. Then we got a residency at the Flamingo. And that was it – because it was a jazz club. GEORGIE FAME

I had my first London job at a very snobby club called the Orchid Room. I had two second-hand dresses, a bedsit in Queen's Gate, something like twelve pounds a week, and I felt absolutely great. I had to sit downstairs in the ladies' loo when I wasn't singing. And when I got up to sing, because I'd developed this little following with my Rodgers and Hart songs no one had heard of, they gave me a little spotlight. So when I got up, I'd switch it on.   ANNIE ROSS

I was sixteen and I got this job singing in a strip club in Manchester. I had this corny little act, and I was called 'Nicole, Our New Song-stress'. You know the sort of thing – an arpeggio, my first note plonked out, and then 'When Madame Pompadour stepped on the ballroom floor . . .' Oh, I often quote from my past, these days, when I'm improvising. I love all the contradictions.   MAGGIE NICOLS

I was being turned into a smart supper club singer. I was in my early twenties. My name was given to me – I accepted it. I had songs chosen for me. The experience was *fundamental* – that introduction into an insincere approach to music – and it was a lesson to me. I don't let anyone tell me what to do any more. Then I came to New York, and I met *the music*. And Max Roach. My life changed at that time. And I knew that I could never go back to what I'd been doing. Or I would be a crazy woman by now.   ABBEY LINCOLN

I was studying law in order to extricate myself from the social cesspool that American Negro people found themselves in at that time. I was a big man on campus, scholastically. Plus, working in a local joint. This also made me a big man on campus. One night the Charlie Parker Quintet came through town for a one-night stand. And since I was very shy, my wife asked Bird if I could scat. Because I'd been doing it. And he said, 'Of course.' So I got on the band-stand and I took about fifteen choruses of something, and I was about to leave the bandstand, and Bird motioned me to sit by him. And he said, 'What do you do?' And I said, 'I'm a law student.' He said, 'You're not going to be a lawyer. You're a jazz singer.' I said, 'I'm studying law because I can't make any money singing jazz.' He said, 'You ought to come to New York and sing jazz.' I said, 'I don't know anybody in New York.' He said, 'You know me.' I said, 'But how could I find you?' And he said, 'Ask anyone.' And, sure enough, two and a half years later, I got out of the bus and went into a phone booth and called Joe Carroll and asked where Bird was and he said, 'The Apollo Bar, 12th Street and 7th Avenue.' And I walked in there and Charlie Parker said, 'Hey, Jon, want to sing some?'   JON HENDRICKS

I was born next door to where Charlie Chaplin was born. My father was an entertainer. He played trumpet and sang and cracked gags. He was black, of course. My mother was Russian. And I was born on St Patrick's Day. So I owe allegiance to the American eagle, the Russian bear and the leprechaun, in that order. When I was twelve, my mother thought her highly polished mahogany furniture was being attacked by death-watch beetle. And she got very worried, until she saw me playing drums with two forks. So to save the furniture, she decided to buy me a set of drums. When I was fifteen, I joined a nightclub band in the West End, because I was big for my age. It was the Nest Club, a legendary place, everybody came down there, Fats Waller, Coleman Hawkins, Art Tatum. I was a drummer until I joined Harry Roy, and he said, 'Can you sing?' And I'd never sung a note in my life, so I said, 'Yes.'   RAY ELLINGTON

I'd always fancied jazz because when I was nine I was given a new saxophone and with it came a record of Coleman Hawkins, playing 'Body and Soul', and my uncle said, 'When you've learnt how to play, that's how you've got to play.' I left school to join a band – straight into the profession when I was fourteen.   BETTY SMITH

My mother wanted me to sing. Singing came before the trumpet. She used to take me around to these talent contests they had in the Los Angeles area at the time. I did it mostly to please her, I guess.
CHET BAKER

I was in school, and I took a job in a cocktail lounge, playing a couple of hours every evening. I was playing classical music from four years old, surrounded by good musicians all the time, hearing nothing but good music. A man used to come in every night to have dinner. One day, around Christmas time, he brought in this gorgeous teddy bear, and he said, 'If you sing "Melancholy Baby", I'll give it to you.' So I sang 'Melancholy Baby'. And from then on I started singing.   SHIRLEY HORN

Around the age of fourteen, fooling around at the piano, I learned to accompany myself in a very rudimentary way. My parents wanted me to get a summer job. And I auditioned for the local radio station, and got my own show, playing and singing, fifteen minutes a week. That was the beginning – it was mostly playing by ear and I got a lot of the harmonies wrong.   CHARLES COCHRAN

You know, the interesting thing that has been happening to me since I've been playing at the Carlyle has been that people are always saying, 'Sing, sing . . .' to me.   BARBARA CARROLL

I like to sing, these days. It rounds me out.   BETTY SMITH

I've studied singing, not jazz singing. If I'd been just a trumpet player, I might be very frustrated. I've always had other things besides music. And jazz. So when they want an older actor who sings and plays jazz trumpet, they ask for me.   BILL DILLARD

I've not been singing in public all that long, maybe five years. I guess I'm doing it to expose my own songs.   DAVE FRISHBERG

I was teaching Marian Montgomery the verse of a song for the very first concert we ever did together. So I sang it through for her, and she said, 'Will you sing it with me on the concert?' And I said, 'I can't.' And I did.   RICHARD RODNEY BENNETT

I'm a musician. I'm not a singer, entertainer, as such. I sing. Because, like most piano players, when I came out of the army after the war, it was singing, singing – the singers had taken over. I had to sing. And I've been doing it ever since.   BOBBY COLE

★

You've got to start somewhere. You might as well fling yourself into sitting in.   PAT SMYTHE

I have been known to get up and sing with anyone.   ANNIE ROSS

I found sitting in very difficult because I was a very shy person. But you just feel you've *got* to.   NORMA WINSTONE

Sitting in is baptism by fire.   MARK MURPHY

When I get on that bandstand to play, it's everything to me. It represents all my knowledge, all my experience. So if *you* come up and sing with me, even for one tune, you're running into my lifetime of music.   SAL MOSCA

I mean, take that young lady last night, who jumped up and offered to sing with me. I didn't want to embarrass anybody, so I invited her up. But, did you notice this? She sang her choruses, then she invited me to take a chorus, so I scatted, because she caught me by surprise. And then she started singing again, and then she said, 'Oh, I'm sorry, I forgot the bass player.' And she gave him space to blow. It showed she was a little bit aware, so it was OK, aside from her nerve. And at least she had the taste not to do a second song.   BOB DOROUGH

Singers are . . . unnecessary? incompetent? Yes, it's a popular theory with musicians. Which singers have to insulate themselves against.   JOHNNY M

70

These people want to sing with you, they come up. It's your gig, you're working, you just want to play your tunes and get your money and go home. And they come up and want to sing. OK, it's a diversion. But, if they show any weakness, there's a real tendency to mess them up. Musicians are perverse, *you* know that. BOB DOROUGH

I'm quite sure I've been in situations where people are trying you out. They throw things at you, just to see what you'll do. JOHNNY M

Well, I've played for singers who couldn't keep the key, you know. And that's a challenge – where the hell did they go? You just follow them. So then it gets to be a game. Like, if they're going to lose the key, I'll *help* them lose it. And you start giving them bizarre changes . . . BOB DOROUGH

Many times, a singer just goes on and starts to sing. And expects you to pick it up, whatever the tune, whatever the key. DAVE FRISHBERG

There's always some singer who wants to sit in with a jazz band. You should acknowledge that you're in a special setting – a *jazz* setting. You're up there with musicians who are capable of making up this fantastic music on the spur of the moment. BOB DOROUGH

They want finished products. First time out, you've got to be Billie Holiday, or you might as well go home. MAGGIE NICOLS

Of course sitting in is daring. How did I equip myself? With *temerity*. You just do it. How did I know *how* to do it? I just knew. How did I know when to come in? I just did. How did I know songs? I just learned them. LEON THOMAS

I can remember the first time. I remember how it felt, and I just loved it. I sang 'Moonlight in Vermont', just the melody, very simply. And I remember changing one note, and that was the first new phrase I ever did. I didn't plan to, but after I did it, it felt so *good*. I was shaking, my legs were shaking, but it felt so good. JAY CLAYTON

I started singing actually at the jam sessions I was running with local musicians. I'd learned some things off records, blues and things. I wasn't very good, but it was a hobby. BERYL BRYDEN

I started by sitting in. I decided to take the plunge and came to London in 1972, knowing no one. I went around asking if I could sing with bands. And, after a while, I didn't have to ask. People knew I was a singer.   SUSANNAH McCORKLE

I started by sitting in with people I knew. I used to hang around Nola's studios, and listen to the bands rehearsing. You know, hide in corners the way most people do, listening to everybody. And thinking, one day *I'm* going to be doing this. So, right from age fifteen or so, whenever I sang, it was always with the finest musicians. They were here and I was here, it was natural at the time.   HELEN MERRILL

If you want to do music, *be around.* You've got to listen. And *listen.* And be part of it. Even if you're not doing it out loud.   JOE WILLIAMS

When I was first singing, in the early fifties, there were some very encouraging musicians, and there were always places to sing. And I had the courage, and it took courage, to get up and sing with these people. They were well known at the time, but now, of course, they're giants. I would really have to be pushed a little – Dizzy *made* me get up and sing one night. And this was always happening. MARILYN MOORE

I've found that the most creative musicians are the ones that are the most excited by seeing potential. They don't stamp on it.   MAGGIE NICOLS

I used to have this ritual. I'd go to a pub where I knew there was music. I wouldn't know a soul there. And I'd arrive, and hear the music going on inside. And the temptation to turn around and go home was always very strong. And I would go in. And it was a bit of a commando operation. You had to introduce yourself to the barman, introduce yourself to the musicians, get them to let you sit in, and then you had to win the public. And come away a *somebody.* JOHNNY M

I used to get a kick out of turning up somewhere where nobody knew me – mind you, I'd be nervous – and asking if I could sit in. Because you could see the immediate reaction with all those men was, 'Oh, no, not another fucking chick singer, oh *fuck.'* And I'd really love to get up and show them that I could do it, *phrase*, and sing and everything.   MAGGIE NICOLS

Joe Marsala called me up, and I sang my two wild choruses of 'Stardust'. Joe's eyes kind of opened up. 'I want to talk to you,' he said, and I was thrilled. I hung around. After they finished, Joe said, 'My budget is such that I can't pay you anything. But if you want to come around, I'll get you up to sing every night. Somebody may hear you and we'll go from there. Maybe if we get enough going here, I can get them to pay you.' Well, I spent eight months, dressed up in a tuxedo every night, from starting time till closing. I sat there for a month without being called once. FRANKIE LAINE

It took him fifteen years of scuffling before he made it. But Frankie never considered giving up any more than I did, even though he was reduced to sleeping on his agent's desk at times. ANITA O'DAY

I guess you might say I was singing for my suppers. But I learned a lot. After that it was a long, long road before I cut 'That's My Desire' the record that sprung me loose in 1947. FRANKIE LAINE

I would get dressed, but not *too* dressed, you know what I mean? Because you're going to be hit on, anyway, no matter how you look at it. That's their priority. All *you* want to do is to be into the music. But you're a *woman*, right? And you're a *singer*. And then, of course, being white – it would have been easier if I'd been black. And then, it's, oh, if only I can just get those words out of my mouth, 'Excuse me, my name is Jay, I'm a singer, could I do a tune?' And they'd say, 'Uh, can you stay around?' And you literally stayed till the last set. And then it was, 'Uh, she wants to sing a tune? What do you want to do?' I would always do simple tunes, and I'd be nervous, but I'd do my couple of choruses. And, sure enough, almost every time, afterwards, they'd be *surprised*. And they'd ask me to do another. That's the test. If I turned one instrumentalist on, or was befriended by one, or got the respect of one, I was already on my way. JAY CLAYTON

★

First time I heard a band, back home in Oklahoma City, it was just the most exciting, thrilling experience I'd ever had. And I said, 'I've just got to be a part of *that*.' MARILYN MOORE

Don't forget that you're stepping into a macho province when you go into music. It's a male-dominated industry. All those girls with the big bands, my God, they really did bite off a *chunk*. Fair enough – put them out in front of the band to look pretty. But they had to *sing*. And live that *life*. On the bus. All those one-nighters. And the guys couldn't treat them as *girl* girls, because familiarity breeds contempt. MARIAN MONTGOMERY

Remember, I was only nineteen years old and Gene Krupa was telling me he'd like to hire me. He was offering me a chance to sing in all the big ballrooms, the top theatres and the radio. And it was one way out of Chicago.   ANITA O'DAY

My sister Betty was fifteen, I was eighteen, so my uncle George went on the road with us. The boys in Tony Pastor's band weren't too thrilled with it. 'What are we, baby sitters here?' We'd done local radio for two years, but we were very young and learning how to do what we did. And it was the passport to instant fame, instant glamour. We were the envy of every girl in the room.   ROSEMARY CLOONEY

Yeah, sitting there, smiling and popping your fingers – yeah! I loved it.   MARILYN MOORE

When we were auditioning for a band singer about thirty girls turned up. Twenty-nine of them sang 'The Lady is a Tramp' all wrong, and the other one sang ''Deed I Do' all on one note. Those were the days the *Melody Maker* described them as 'hip chirpers'. We had the audition, really, so that the band could have a good laugh.   RONNIE SCOTT

Ronnie's band? Oh my gosh, oh those terrible stories, Kitty, they're all *true*. It was a monster band. They gave me a terrible time. They're nice to me now, but they were all Angry Young Men in those days, and *purist*. They didn't want a singer at all, really. They wanted to play their jazz. I used to get so upset, but I would never let them see me get upset. If I had a little weep, I used to go away and weep on my own.   BARBARA JAY

People were very distracted by drugs and alcohol in those days. And there were all these little groupies hanging round the bandstand. The band could be very teasing, especially if you kept yourself to yourself and didn't get involved with any of them.   MARILYN MOORE

My wife was singing with one of the bands I worked with. And if any of the musicians gave *her* a hard time, she'd kick his music stand over.   KENNY CLARE

Travelling with the Basie band was pretty nice. Probably the biggest problem was finding a bathroom when I needed one, particularly in the South. Sometimes we'd stay with friends, because the hotels were so bad. I used to cook for a lot of the guys. I carried my little hotplate around, and when we played theatres, the dressing-room would be the kitchen.   HELEN HUMES

It is strange that one of the most vital members of the Fats Waller group is seldom mentioned. She is Myra Johnson, the dynamic singer who stuck through thick and thin with the band, staying with it right to the end. Myra, a diminutive sepia bombshell, could rival her big partner in putting over a song and could whip up an audience into a frenzy with her blues and rhythm singing . . . She soon became invaluable in many ways. She acted as nursemaid, with medicine and pills, when any of the boys fell ill, and her voluminous travelling-bag always contained such essentials as needle, thread and stocking caps. She quickly earned the admiration and companionship of the whole band, and, except by Fats, who was apt to call her anything under the sun as the mood suited him, she was known as just plain 'Johnson' by the entire crew. As she felt more and more secure in her job, she was inclined to talk to outsiders about it – about how much the band liked and depended on her. 'I'm the sweetheart of the whole band,' she confided to some fellow standing round the bandstand at a dance. She did not realize that she had been overheard, until later that night, en route to Pittsburgh in a Pullman. The berths had all been made up and the gang was sitting around in the aisle in dressing-gowns, passing a bottle from hand to hand. Pretty soon, Myra, fairly drowsy, flopped back into her berth and drew the curtains. To a man, the band got to their feet, and advancing on the hapless girl's bunk, threw aside the curtains and jumped one after another on top of the tiny form. 'So you're the sweetheart of the band, eh, Johnson?' they cried. 'Isn't it wonderful?'   ED KIRKEBY

Travelling on a band bus, there would be sections. There would be the booze section, and then there would be the grass section. And then a couple of times we had some that stayed way at the back – and I think they were on everything but roller-skates.   ROSEMARY CLOONEY

I'd started singing professionally at nineteen, and I'd had five years with Claude Thornhill. But I'd set my sights on the Kenton band. And it happened. June Christy heard me on a radio broadcast and she was leaving the band. I had that low-voiced sound the Kenton band needed. A lot of people sent in demos. But I got the job. It was my first big break.   CHRIS CONNOR

When I started I was so raw and inexperienced. I'd only sung in local

75

pubs and dances. I'd done all these auditions and talent contests and never won anything. And I was sort of, well, not depressed, but resigned to the idea that it was going to have to be just a hobby for the rest of my life. But when I auditioned for John Dankworth and the Seven, the fact that I wasn't singing like Doris Day or the current fashionable singer was one of the appealing things to them. And that's probably why I didn't pass the other auditions, either.
CLEO LAINE

I just sort of, fell into it. As a kid in Milwaukee, when I used to listen to the radio, I never dreamed I'd be doing it. Here was I, working. I couldn't believe my luck. Here I was, travelling round the country with all these great musicians.   JACKIE CAIN

I was frightened to death of the musicians. It was a dream come true, and frightening, both, really. I'd never been with real jazzers before. After hiring me because I was different, after a while they started telling me to listen to other singers. And I felt terribly hurt and angry about it. Because I felt I should discover *myself* in some way.   CLEO LAINE

What you had to do was deliver what you were required to deliver every night, on the dot.   ROSEMARY CLOONEY

Musicians were unkind to budding vocalists. Really, in those days, a singer was a sex symbol, sitting there all night to attract people. But the Seven wanted a good singer, she could look like anything as long as she could sing. But in the end they realized that they wanted both, a good singer *and* a sex symbol. And I never did quite achieve that for them.   CLEO LAINE

You sat in the corner all night. And the thing was 'What *style* am I going to develop in front of the microphone?' You had to stand like *this*. And you thought, do I keep my hands at my sides? Do I hold the base of the mike with one hand? Do I move? And we'd all sit with our legs crossed and our hands like *this*. There was a way band singers were supposed to look.   BARBARA JAY

They really were rough times. We used to do vaudeville theatres. And on the weekends, we'd do five or six shows a day, in between the movies. On one-nighters, the band would play four hours a night, and a singer would do maybe twenty songs. And no rest. You just get into the bus after the gig, sleeping in the seat, and on to the next place.   BILL DILLARD

76

I wouldn't know what town I was in. You're moving so fast. I'd wake in a hotel and I wouldn't know where I *was*.   CHRIS CONNOR

Alcohol can take the place of nutrition, it kills your appetite. It also gives a false sense of energy.   MARILYN MOORE

And some of the guys were on the road for years and years. It really is a wonder anyone got through it as a healthy human being.   CHRIS CONNOR

Eventually it can wear you down – that constant moving, setting up, fast bite to eat, show, tearing down, moving on, get a little sleep, next one . . .   ROY KRAL

I finally became very ill and Stan wasn't at all sympathetic because he was holding up and he felt if he was, everyone else should be, too.   JUNE CHRISTY

I had six years of one-nighters in all, and that was enough. I quit Stan because I was exhausted. Maybe I should have stayed longer to gain more of a name for myself but I felt if I didn't get off the road, I was going to crack up.   CHRIS CONNOR

I believe with Nietzsche, 'What doesn't kill you, makes you stronger.' MARILYN MOORE

4
Who With?

. . . they talk about the jazz musicians they work with.
And the jazz musicians talk about them . . .

Song is the first. Music is the accompaniment of song. Song is the voice and the human being. Music, you might say, is the *shadow* of song. So, whenever you're singing, you overshadow the music. And the instrumentalists. Some regret it. Some don't. Some like accompanying you. Some do not.   LEON THOMAS

Bruce Turner always said he's jealous of singers. He says he plays a marvellous solo and the audience doesn't even notice it. And then a singer gets up and doesn't do anything but sing the song, and gets all the applause.   JOHNNY M

When I was working with Frank Weir in England, we had a singer who had a voice, but . . . And I wrote some arrangements she sang. And she said, 'Oh, that's the way the band should *sound* behind a singer.' And I said, 'Are you telling me, with *your* limited ability, how to write for you?' And she said, 'Oh, no, not at all.' 'I'll tell you what the problem is,' I said. 'We musicians don't like being told what to do by someone who came into the business by making eyes at the bandleader.' *I put her in her place.*   GEORGE SHEARING

Every time I made a mistake, this guy would just turn round and say things like, 'Do you always go around dropping beats?' Or, 'Your intonation is terrible.' And I'd go home and cry.   MAGGIE NICOLS

Jazz musicians resent the lack of musicianship in singers. Not only the lack of it, but the *acclaim* of the public for it.   BOBBY TUCKER

Singers get paid more. They don't have to work so hard to sharpen their craft. Singers don't have the same pressure to be *excellent*, see, that horn players have.   MARION COWINGS

Half of these singers can't even read a top line.   GEORGE SHEARING

Crosby didn't read a note. Judy Garland didn't even know the key she sang 'Over the Rainbow' in.   CHARLES COCHRAN

Because musicians have learned to read the notes, they think the *music* is in the notes.   ABBEY LINCOLN

Billie Holiday wasn't a quick learner. But, it's like the highly polished singers who work in studios – they are the epitome of *musicians*. But, as for depth of feeling, you know – well, you don't have *time* to feel. You just sight read anything and put it down and go on to something else.   BOBBY TUCKER

I mean, I can sight read like I read a book, but that's nothing to do with singing a song.   RICHARD RODNEY BENNETT

Musicians who say singers are ill-equipped are looking at it just from the viewpoint of being able to sight read music, and maybe improvise, things like that. Whereas there are other aspects to singing, you know, like the *words*, the sound, the stories, the emotional content, all that.   JACKIE CAIN

It takes a long time to learn a song and to *understand* the song.
ABBEY LINCOLN

Generally speaking, singers are show business people. Jazz musicians always have an aversion to show business types – I know I do. Early in your career you learn to discriminate between what's done for show, and what's done because the person feels like doing it.   MOSE ALLISON

Ralph Sharon says his autobiography is going to be called *I Saw Their Backs*.   PAT SMYTHE

Singers are going to be aiming at stardom and the public accepts them. And a musician will spend a lifetime learning his craft and practising *forever*. And then someone will come in, with no training, no background, and take all the money.   BOBBY TUCKER

They get the limo and you get the bus.   JIMMY ROWLES

I hate to generalize, but take the success of Frank Sinatra. Frank was the male vocalist with Tommy Dorsey. And I guarantee that those musicians still have to grovel to make a living, whereas he can probably buy the Chase National Bank. He's paid dues, sure. But do you think he paid more than, say, the piano player with Tommy Dorsey? Or Charlie Shavers?   BOBBY TUCKER

What I hated when I was a full-time professional accompanist for singers – it's decades ago now – was the singer imposing on me all his or her insecurities about music and depositing it all in my lap.   DAVE FRISHBERG

Most singers are a peculiar mixture of egomania and insecurity.   PAT SMYTHE

If I walked on a bandstand and I didn't really know what was going on, I'd feel insecure too.   SAL MOSCA

There's a lot of insecurity about you being a *woman*, that's in these men's attitudes to singers.   MAGGIE NICOLS

Singers feel paranoid around musicians because most musicians have studied, and singers haven't.   MAL WALDRON

It's so hard to back up and go back to musical kindergarten and learn all these things, when you really want to sing. You're so damn spoiled. You're so used to that immediacy – immediate gratification.
MARILYN MOORE

When you're a young musician, you don't realize that the singer must have support. Yes, you must give her support. If she dumps a little bit on you – and I say, 'she' because it usually is, but not necessarily – you have to understand the pressure that person is under. Generally ill-equipped. And up there as a focal point.
BOBBY COLE

I've always found that the greater a musician is, the more supportive he is. Because he can afford to be.   MARILYN MOORE

The more equipped a musician is, the less she will detonate *his* insecurities.   BOBBY COLE

When singers moan, 'Oh, musicians don't seem to like singers', I say, 'Think about it.' If you go along and you don't know what speed you want to do the thing at, you don't know how many bars intro, and you don't know what key, they can't take you seriously, can they?   NORMA WINSTONE

Sometimes, before you have the confidence to do what you want to

do, and the *authority*, you plant seeds of doubt in everybody else.
ELAINE DELMAR

You must always do what you want to do. Because if you start adjusting to the group, without presenting any challenge to them, the job becomes boring to them. They love challenges, as well.   JOE WILLIAMS

You can't be giving them the same old licks over and over. You have to surprise them.   PETER DEAN

You have to make your statement.   ELAINE DELMAR

If you can make your musical statement strongly and with conviction, whether they agree with it or not, then they have something to build with. Say you go up and say, 'I'm a singer. I'd like to sing "Stardust" in B flat.' They don't know what you're going to do. So, everybody's just laying back and waiting to see what might be the best way to accompany you. But if *you're* waiting to see what *they're* going to do, so *you* have a direction, then you get into the 'Who's waiting for who?' bind.   SAL MOSCA

I like singers who are so confident and so easy with what they do that a change of tempo or feeling is not going to throw them, or ruin the song. Singers ought to be able to do that, my gosh, musicians do.   DAVE FRISHBERG

I've always been in control of my music. I worked with big bands at the Apollo Theater at the beginning. I told the arranger how I wanted it. There was a conductor, but he got his time from me. He watched *me*. You need to be tough if your music is different. And if you want it to remain that way. And if you don't want them to control *you*.   BETTY CARTER

Most of the singers I've worked with are repetitious. They do the same songs, the same way, every night. As a result, the accompaniment has to be the same way every night – every night the way that it happened on the *best* night.   GRADY TATE

There's a totality that makes a performance – the love affair between you, your musicians and your audience.   SYLVIA SYMS

You need a good marriage. I know within sixteen bars whether we're going to be married or not. It's a mysterious thing, isn't it?   GEORGE SHEARING

It's all got to *mesh*. It's all making *music*.   JOE WILLIAMS

I make myself part of them. I make them part of me. Musicians are ninety per cent of Jimmy Witherspoon. And I always express that. If a musician plays something I like, I look at him and show him I like it.   JIMMY WITHERSPOON

Once I worked in a club here and I sang a chorus and then stood back to let the piano player take a chorus. And the manager said, 'You know that song was going so well till you forgot the words.' SUSANNAH McCORKLE

I like musicians to play behind me while I'm singing. And I like them to take solos. Then I step out of the picture, to the side, and I do a few little steps in the dark, and just sway a bit. Then I just *float* over to the centre and start again.   ADELAIDE HALL

An arrangement should be a happening, you know.   ABBEY LINCOLN

You can start out with nothing but a tune and the people playing with you. And you can move right *out*, and come right back, and in the end you've *made* a little arrangement. Nothing written down. That's jazz. And it's so exciting.   ADELAIDE HALL

And then every musician you work with is different. You get different things going, on the same tunes.   SHEILA JORDAN

And with first-rate musicians you don't have any trouble at all. Because they *feel* what you're doing. You sort of send messages to each other, you know? You feel each other, musically. It's a wonderful feeling.   ADELAIDE HALL

That's why you try to work with good musicians, because they have that kind of innate sense of what should happen.   JACKIE CAIN

You don't explain anything to good musicians. I don't have to go through the whole song. I give them the tempo, and we do the intro. Then we do the end – top and tail it. You sort of sketch it – who's going to do what, where.   ADELAIDE HALL

Rehearsal isn't the crucial thing with me. The right feeling is the crucial thing with me.   JOE WILLIAMS

I work out a skeleton arrangement with the piano player. Then put on the meat in performance.   JOE LEE WILSON

I know people who rehearse themselves to death before the show – that's because you like to hear the sound of your own voice. And

when they get on stage they find they can't make the notes.   JOE
WILLIAMS

I've been involved in performances which were miraculous, with no
rehearsal at all. On the other hand, I've been involved in performances with no rehearsal at all, which have been disastrous. You
can never know what makes a better performance.   PAT SMYTHE

Mabel Mercer would work on her songs by constantly going over
them, over and over and over. I hated to go to rehearsal with her,
because we'd do one tune all day.   JIMMY LYON

Sure, musicians will rehearse things over and over, because they
want the job. Then they'll go home and curse, or get out in their cars
and bitch about it. But while you're there, they'll put on a smile and
say, 'Oh, try it again, one more time. Oh, you want it this way?' Bla
bla bla. But it's all false, it's all phoney. And then, if you say, 'Well,
it's not *quite* . . . why don't you play like so and so?' Or even
bring out a record and say, 'Why don't you play like this?' It's
unreal.   SAL MOSCA

You have to be able to get the musicians going, get them warmed
up, so they enjoy their playing, that's your job. It's not your job to
annoy them. Don't give them that temperamental business. Because
they'll play for you, but it won't be as *sweet.*   ADELAIDE HALL

The biggest thrill is when something unexpected *happens.* And it's
sparked off by you, or one of the other musicians. And you feel it's
working. And you feel, this is what it should be like all the time.
And you feel, why can't it be like this more often? You try to analyse
it – *why*, how did it happen? And if you try to set it up again, it won't
happen. Not the same way. And perhaps after a couple of gos at it,
perhaps it won't happen at all.   NORMA WINSTONE

★

It's an art, being an accompanist.   ANNIE ROSS

Being an accompanist is a *vocation.* And it's not the same as being a
soloist.   RICHARD RODNEY BENNETT

I mean, not every great piano player is a great accompanist.   ANNIE
ROSS

Sometimes you hear someone wonderful. And you think he's so
wonderful, we'll be wonderful *together.* And then you get together
and it's awful. And it isn't that he can't play and that you can't sing.

84

It's just that the magic doesn't happen.   SHEILA JORDAN

There's a lot of piano players who are just focused on being very *pianistic*. And a lot of them are very involved with technique, and are unable to get out of themselves long enough to be open to what someone else is doing. They don't seem to be sensitive to your phrasing. Or realize that they're cutting into your phrasing, cutting into the inflection or the quality of it, the time, or the shading. They just barge right in and cut right through, with the overtones of the piano, with too much volume, with too much technique overpowering you, with an inability to communicate.   MARILYN MOORE

Like, some piano players close my ears up completely.   MARK MURPHY

Some of these cats, they think you can take these standard songs and add these extended chords. They have a resentment for anything that's simple. They want to make it all so difficult.   MAXINE SULLIVAN

These days, I want *less* than they're prepared to give me. I want everything so simple, when I'm singing, that it's almost non-existent. If you say, 'Less, less, less', they think you're kind of putting them down.   ROSEMARY CLOONEY

I used to ask Jimmy Jones, when he was Sarah's accompanist, what his secret was. And he said, 'When she's *not* singing, that's when I play.'   MARILYN MOORE

You listen to the way a singer likes to sing, and then you complement him or her in the spaces that naturally occur in what they're doing.   DIGBY FAIRWEATHER

I remember playing for Teddi King before she died. And it was as though we'd been working together for months. It was like *breathing* together. And it wasn't as though I was close to her as a person, and I didn't know her singing very well. But you can get extraordinary contact with some singers.   RICHARD RODNEY BENNETT

It's a question of trying to bring out the best in them by what you do. It's just an instinctive thing.   PAT SMYTHE

I like women and I like to play for them. In general, I'm a very good singers' pianist. I support them, and I know the words and I know the songs, and I know the right keys for singers. But, every now and again, you get a singer who regards pianists as being completely interchangeable. All he or she wants is someone to play the song at exactly the tempo they're used to, with exactly the same pauses for breath, and so on. And they're not at all interested in making music *with* a pianist.   RICHARD RODNEY BENNETT

I've had a couple of disastrous experiences with lady singers. Sometimes they just know they're dissatisfied, but they can't tell you what they want. Sometimes they just don't like you, and that's *it*.   BOB DOROUGH

Each singer is quite different. Some people know exactly what they're going to do before they do it. There's Blossom Dearie, who knows to the last note what she's going to do, and has, in fact, worked on her accompaniments for months. But it doesn't make the finished result any less good than people like Anita O'Day and Annie Ross, who never know from one moment to the next what they're going to sing. Some really know what they're doing. Others can *not* know, and be just as demanding. You work by trial and error.   PAT SMYTHE

I ask them if they're comfortable. I find I usually know their key, the extent of their range, and the extent and range of the song. If I'm speaking to a musician-singer, I'll say, 'Suppose we try it in five sharps?' That's double-Dutch to a non-musician-singer, so I say, 'You want it a little bit lower?' Then, if they know what they're doing, they might say, 'When we come to the second bridge, I'd like to try it rubato.' Fine, that gives me a chance to play some different harmonies. And, if they're musicians, they're overjoyed by that, rather than being thrown because it's not what they're used to hearing. This is the thing about a musician-singer.   GEORGE SHEARING

Singers are always looking for pianists. People don't stay together for ever. You go your ways. Music is very transitory.   SAL MOSCA

Like Abbey Lincoln says, 'There's always another good one out there somewhere.'   MARILYN MOORE

Look, there are such things as lousy musicians. Cats who just can't play, period. And it's no use saying, 'Look, man, let's do it right next time.' So for that week I suffer. Go in my dressing-room and read. Or go out and get loaded, so I just don't *care*.   MAXINE SULLIVAN

If you don't have your own group, you often have to change what you would like to do, because it can't be done. So you have to find out what they know. Sometimes you pull out your music and they just can't play it. So you're going to sound horrible and it's going to sound like it's your fault. So, rather than sounding horrible, you say, 'Hey, man, what do you know that *I* might know?'   JOE LEE WILSON

Some of them can read music, but not when you put it in front of them, know what I mean? And some of them don't want to put on their glasses to read music. So I have in my pocket a list of about twenty-five songs, with the keys. Sometimes they'll only know five. Then I have to think of some standards just out of my head, that everybody ought to know. The man is not paying me to go in there and do trite songs, but you're stuck. Then I really have to get into the clown act. I think of things to say. I take up a lot of time between numbers. I go around and ask if anyone's having a birthday, and we do 'Happy Birthday to You', or I get them singing with me or something like that. *Shooooooooo!*   MAXINE SULLIVAN

I went out and sat in last night, and there were these really schooled British guys – people like Brian Lemon. And I said, 'How about – ?' And they knew it. And I said, 'Give me a C chord.' And they did. And it was fine. And I didn't know I was going there. And I didn't know they were playing there. And they didn't know I was coming. And we'd never rehearsed. And we didn't need to rehearse. Anywhere in the world you can do that. And jazz is the only thing it can happen in.   MARK MURPHY

You know, sometimes it'll be really rough. And then maybe the next gig, you get the cream, the best. You can relax, and it all comes out good. Everything sounds good. The musicians sound good. You sound better than you ever thought you could sound. So these are the *ups*. And maybe it's better that it doesn't happen more often than it does, or you'd get carried away and expect too much. And then you'd run into one of those bummers, and you *really* want to die.   MAXINE SULLIVAN

★

If you marry a piano player, you may think you're solving a problem.   PEPI LEMER

Roy's sister Irene used to say, 'Oh God, *every* musician you meet – everyone's wife is a singer. And usually bad.'   JACKIE CAIN

They generally marry a piano player or a bass player or a drummer or someone that can pull the rhythm section together when they're on the road. They're marriages of convenience. Because the person is lonely on the road.   MILT GABLER

Singers marry musicians because they're *there*.   ANNIE ROSS

I know when I started out I never really wanted to do this alone, be on the road, a girl on the make, trying to get success, you know. You have to be so aggressive and so unpleasant. I always wanted to share it with somebody. So the way it happened with Roy was perfect. We've been married thirty-five years, this year. And people say, 'How can you stand to be together twenty-four hours a day?' I'd find it harder wondering what he was up to if he were someplace else.
JACKIE CAIN

I would hate to think what would have happened if I'd had to hack it out on my own. I think if you have one musician you can rely on, someone you can battle with, someone you know well enough *to* battle with, you can make progress. I know what I want, musically. John knows what he wants. I need someone I can yell at and be yelled back at, but to know that in the end he's not going to walk out on me.   CLEO LAINE

Stanley was my knight in shining armour. He could do no wrong. The romance started right after we went on the road. I didn't want anybody to know. He had hired me as a singer, on my talent. I had never been the kind of singer to get involved with bandleaders, like some singers do . . . Then bit by bit we started travelling in the car, and everybody kind of caught on because we were staying together in hotels and everything . . . I was attracted to the man's misery, partly. And I really thought that if he had a home and a family and somebody to love him, he'd be happy.   ANN RICHARDS

It wasn't so easy being married to John Kirby, you know. With 'Loch Lomond' I was known nationally, internationally, in fact. And his band really wasn't. But after a while we were separated by the work. The record was so big. And you know all the booking agents aren't going to let you stay home in one place, they're going to get that loot while they can. So the time that you're together gets narrower and narrower. And the next thing you know, you're not seeing each other at all.   MAXINE SULLIVAN

When I married, I had to give up what I probably really felt the deepest passion for. Up to that time, the musicians I'd been

Susannah McCorkle

Pepi Lemer

Norma Winstone

Annie Ross

Johnny M

Marian Montgomery and Richard Rodney Bennett

Digby Fairweather

Sheila Jordan

Adelaide Hall

Trummy Young

Joe Lee Wilson

Carrie Smith

Cleo Laine and John Dankworth

Jackie Cain and Roy Kral

Bobby Short

Barbara Jay

Peter Dean

Marion Cowings

Elaine Delmar

George Melly

Georgie Fame

Jay Clayton

Al Jarreau

Ray Charles and Billy Eckstine

Leon Thomas

Betty Carter

Jimmy Witherspoon

Helen Merrill

Marilyn Moore

Slim Gaillard

Mose Allison

Sylvia Syms

Bobby McFerrin   Joe Williams

Beryl Bryden and Billie Holiday

Ray Ellington

Charles Cochran

involved with had been very supportive. And I suppose I fantasized that marrying a musician like Al, it would be the same way. But my choice was very poor in terms of how we understood our rôles and our priorities. He didn't want me to sing and he did everything he could to discourage me. And he succeeded. I ended up out of it, raising two small children, virtually alone, for, I guess the next fifteen, eighteen years. And I really didn't get to sing all that time.   MARILYN MOORE

They fall in love with you because of what you do. And then they want to stop you doing it.   CARRIE SMITH

I call it 'capturing the mermaid'. It happens a lot. I know *that* one.   JEANNE LEE

Stanley was very fearful of marriage. I was so in love with him that I wanted to give up my career and raise a family. Five kids. He said, 'I'll do anything to help you in your career', and I said, 'I don't want my career any more. I want to get married. I love you and I'll make you a happy home.' I guess I had delusions of having him home with me.   ANN RICHARDS

Nobody was happy about it. Ann was the downfall of the band. From then on things really changed. How could he relax? How could he be like he was? None of us liked her. She wasn't classy at all. She was climbing. She just wanted to be Mrs Stan Kenton; she didn't really want to be a wife to him. The minute she married him, she quit singing.   MEL LEWIS

I got back into singing and went back on the road myself to get away from the marriage. And I did get this tremendous, burning desire to sing again, because my ego had gotten to be about the size of a pinhead. I used to wonder, why did he ever marry me? He didn't want me to change, or grow. He always treated me like a little girl. I kept blaming myself for everything . . . And I *missed* my singing: that was where my identity was sort of wrapped up . . . I loved the children and I really enjoyed being a mother, but *it wasn't enough for me*. I'd only go out for three weeks at a time, spasmodically. In a town where I was singing, at least there was a little glamour involved, and I could go out and be with people, and even date and screw around if I wanted to. I was escaping, just like he was.   ANN RICHARDS

Men can do it, be in the business, leave their wives, go on the road, come back, and they can have wives that will stick to the bitter end, you know. A lot of wives still don't mind playing that part, being supportive. But it isn't easy for a man to be supportive of a woman out there in the limelight.   MAXINE SULLIVAN

If two people are professional musicians, and both are doing *different* things, it's hard for them to share a strong relationship. JACKIE CAIN

Kirby and I were divorced. It's not a pleasant experience, after all those *hopes*, you know.   MAXINE SULLIVAN

I was a jazz groupie before the word was invented. I was always in love with musicians peripherally. Peripherally – because I think I was never cute enough for them to want to make it otherwise. But I was very brave and I wanted to know everything about everything. So I had a very full and very varied education in music.   SYLVIA SYMS

I was desperate to sing, desperate, desperate. And I'd get terribly romantically carried away by the music, and what I thought was the soul of the person playing and get *crushes*. I had no confidence. Plus, they had the idea that I was just a chick who was a total pushover, that they could get to service them sexually in any way whatsoever. And what amazes me now is that I allowed myself to do that. But I realize now that I was so desperate to be popular and be liked and be part of the jazz thing.   MAGGIE NICOLS

You go through a lot of stages of wanting to be one of the boys. I go through a lot of changes emotionally, with trying to work with men, musicians, and what I think of as my masculine energy. And trying to get them to take me seriously, which they do now.   JULIE AMIET

In fact, a lot of musicians to this day, see me as one of the boys. It's funny, when you sort of bask in male approval and you're afraid of losing it. So then you get into competition with other female singers, and you feel threatened, and you *want* to hear bad things said about them and all sorts of stuff. I'd be in the band van and I'd be sort of *co-opted* into being an honorary boy when they made all those horrible remarks about women.   MAGGIE NICOLS

You don't get closer to the music by getting closer to a musician, necessarily. Duke Jordan was playing with Charlie Parker and one of the reasons I went out with him was because I wanted to get closer to Bird. I was such a Bird freak when I was a kid – ooh, that *Bird*.   SHEILA JORDAN

When I made that album, I hadn't sung for four years. I had four weeks' rehearsal with the piano player, and then Al told me just about a week before I did the album that he just really didn't like the way I sang. And he didn't want to be on it. Which is not too encouraging for someone getting ready to make their first album. Pretty *devastating*.   MARILYN MOORE

I met my husband on sessions and stuff. We were friends, and that's how it happened. It helped me, too. Being married made my life easier, when I look back, in terms of getting hit on by the others and things, I escaped some of that. I mean, you still get hit on, it's still women and men, but there was a certain protection.   JAY CLAYTON

I think I found out very early on that it's a great mistake to have an affair with any of the musicians in the band you're singing with. And also, you've got to beware of band wives.   BERYL BRYDEN

It's funny being married to a piano player, often they won't play for you. I mean, when I married Cliff he played for his own groups most of the time. He didn't play for me, even around the house.   MAXINE SULLIVAN

I married Duke who never even encouraged me when I sang. He had to be *told* I could sing.   SHEILA JORDAN

It certainly helps me to be married to a piano player. I find it useful because John writes things out for me, apart from anything else. Usually we have the same taste. I'm obviously more openly critical of him and he is of me, than we would be if we weren't married. You're more careful and polite with other people. I think I've opened his eyes to a lot about songs. And also the value of actually *learning* songs, learning what words and tunes *are*. And obviously, I've learned a hell of a lot from him.   NORMA WINSTONE

Being married to Jack is terribly helpful. He's a very good bass player. And he's very good at sorting out songs for me, he knows what suits me. He's very understanding, a tower of strength, as they say.   BETTY SMITH

André Persiany was a great piano player and he got me into singing ad lib tempo verses, which I'd never done before. And I had my first affair with a Frenchman with him.   BERYL BRYDEN

The first musician who helped me in any practical way was this piano player called Denis Rose. I saw him floating about, looking all pale and thin, hollow cheeks, and those eyes, beautiful Denis.

And he was like an older brother or a father or something. And he did sort of take me under his wing. He knew exactly what key I should sing in. And he'd start by making it very easy for me, and when he thought I was developing a bit, he'd make it more difficult. And then he'd try to actually catch me out, but if I tripped, he'd always be there to catch me. He was wonderful, because he never saw me as a slag or anything. If I hadn't met someone like Denis . . .   MAGGIE NICOLS

Of course, I'm very happy that I met Keith Ingham, because he loved songs, and he wasn't really doing very much. I had that American spirit of forging ahead, communicating to people, making something of what I could do. And he didn't really have that at all. So we really complemented each other. He used to play piano at home a lot. And I wanted to perform, work, be a singer, make records, I wanted to sing to people. So we helped each other a lot. And, for the years we were together, we spent all our time learning songs. We were not a very well-matched couple at all. But I think neither of us has any regrets for those years. Because we started doing it for the love of music, we really just gave everything to music. And now we have a lot to show for it.   SUSANNAH McCORKLE

Jazz musicians give you the truth. Instead of just playing the music, they give you *them*. If they like you.   JULIE AMIET

The musicians who were really supportive, I'd like to name. There were Ray Bryant and Phineas Newborn, who used to come out to my house and play. And this wasn't for a job and it wasn't for sex, it was nothing other than the sheer joy of playing and singing together. Wynton Kelly was always over, probably my most productive years were with him. Teddy Wilson used to drive over to my gigs, just to be there.   MARILYN MOORE

Black people, black musicians, told me I could sing. I used to sing as a little kid in school and white people used to *laugh* at me. But when I sang in clubs in Detroit I got only encouragement.   SHEILA JORDAN

I started to work with the local coloured musicians – another thing that shocked people in the South. But they weren't quite sure whether I was 'passing' or not, because of the voice I had.   MARIAN MONTGOMERY

I sang my songs. And I was accepted by black musicians as few white singers were. By my *idols*. I don't think I knew how lucky I was.   ANNIE ROSS

You know, for the first time in my life now, I'm involved with a musician. And I keep thinking, why has it taken so *long*?   ELAINE DELMAR

Anyway, I can tell you now that musical intimacy is on a completely different plane – deeper, longer-lasting, better than the steamiest sexual liaison. Passion wears out, but the longer you work with a really rhythmical, inventive, swinging musician, the closer you become.   ANITA O'DAY

Musicians can be very protective. But if they don't like you, they will let you know, no doubt about it. They can be some of the best friends you can have on the road. I know most of them. I know most of the wives. I know most of the girlfriends. But I know musicians. And they treat me like I'm their sister. Because they know they *better* do that. I haven't seen any musician that I'd want in my life. Because, like I say, *I know musicians*.   CARRIE SMITH

Sometimes musicians can help you. Sometimes they need help themselves.   ABBEY LINCOLN

5
What? And What Not

. . . they talk about the words and music they sing. And
about singing without words . . .

About every six months I hear a song and I say, 'I've got to have
that. That belongs to *me*.'   RICHARD RODNEY BENNETT

Songs just seem to come to me at the right time.   JULIE AMIET

If jazz singers don't have anything else going for them, they usually
have excellent taste in songs. They just don't sing a dumb tune.
SHEILA JORDAN

There are jazz musicians who are song fans. And there are singers
who are song fans. And there are jazz musicians who aren't song
fans. And there are singers who aren't song fans. Many, many
singers are more interested in their own image than they are in the
songs they are singing. They look for things that show off the voice,
or display their virtuosity, or their personality. That's the nature of
the business. Some of the people it attracts aren't necessarily
interested in music.   DAVE FRISHBERG

It's hard to find songs that mean a lot to me. I guess you'd say, 'Now,
come on, Ray, with all the thousands and thousands of songs, how
can that be?' But it's true. When I say I have trouble finding songs, I
don't mean I have trouble finding good songs, but I have trouble
finding good songs for *me*.   RAY CHARLES

The only people in this business who make any money are the songwriters. So you have to be careful who you give the money *to*.   JOE
LEE WILSON.

I'm not really into the process of looking for songs. I would rather write them myself. Or just improvise.   BOBBY McFERRIN

The core of my work is the songs that I write. I express as best I can how it feels to be here on this planet, at this time, with these people.   ABBEY LINCOLN

I like to sing songs by my composer friends. I get them to play it on a tape for me and sing it, even if they can't sing. And I sing it in their key, with their feeling.   JOE LEE WILSON

There are so many songs that are better than I am.   PETER DEAN

I don't sing songs I *can't* sing. I don't want to strain, I don't want to have to be rooting for notes. I have a limited range. There's lots of good music I *hear*, but not for me to sing.   MAXINE SULLIVAN

Now, the way I choose material has always been by the way I feel for a song. The song awakens or detonates something inside of me.   BOBBY COLE

Sometimes I hear a song – any kind of a song – and I can *feel* that song, I can feel the way I sing *singing* that song.   SHEILA JORDAN

I sing songs that I can live, that I can get inside, and make you dream when you hear them. You understand what I'm saying?   SALENA JONES

I sing songs of my vintage. I sing love songs. I think love and love-making are the most important things in the world.   SYLVIA SYMS

I like to sing a song that I can put some of myself into.   CHRIS CONNOR

If it's something I don't like, I never do it very well. That's why I only sing things I like.   BETTY SMITH

I feel that I use my songs to expose a lot of things I would be too shy to expose in a first meeting. But I'm getting that together, too, gradually trusting my own feelings more.   MARION COWINGS

The songs can tell your life story for you, can't they?   ADELAIDE HALL

Sure, I choose songs to suit various sides of my nature – wearing your heart on your sleeve, laughing at life, being amused by some things, being hurt by some things. I think you must have a mixture of feelings, of living.   SYLVIA SYMS

I look for songs that I feel I can empathize with – that's the ambiva-
lent, edgy, working-out-your-contradictions things. My songs are
my therapy, I'm sure.   MOSE ALLISON

I'm sure a lot of people live out their fantasy life on stage.   MARION
COWINGS

★

I always looked for songs that had a simple lyric, with an *idea*.
Simple songs, that would be good because the band could *swing*
them.   MAXINE SULLIVAN

Of course, being a musician, I suppose the first thing I listen to is the
melodic line, to see what it says, where it's going. And then I listen
to the lyric and see what kind of story is being told. Words and music
are a marriage.   BILLY ECKSTINE

I'm pretty much a tune and chord man in my heart. That's what
turns me on, always. And lyrics that *sing* well, not too many consonants.   CHARLES COCHRAN

Choosing songs? Strangely enough, I go *back*. The older the song,
the more likely it is to appeal to me.   ELAINE DELMAR

I have found some wonderful *new* songs, too, but I have problems
with my young jazz musicians, because they're kind of reverse
snobs. They don't want to play anything new. They've decided all
the songs written before 1950 were perfect.   ROSEMARY CLOONEY

You can always go back to the standards, which are always there.
And sometimes you can go back to how it was originally done, and
it's quite shocking for an audience. Like singing 'How High the
Moon' as a ballad.   CLEO LAINE

Certain standards are so well constructed you're constantly amazed
how good they are.   MARK MURPHY

You know what happens, things go in cycles. Suddenly every singer-
player is doing a certain tune, something obscure a year or so ago is
no longer obscure.   BARBARA CARROLL

Of course, a popular song is the expression of the moment – to begin
with.   BOBBY COLE

The twenties songs are quite down to earth, particularly the ones
that come from the black culture. When the Depression struck,

popular music seemed more escapist, all about dreams. DIGBY
FAIRWEATHER

A lot of popular songs are painting pictures that aren't there.
Nothing to do with real life. 'CLEANHEAD' VINSON

Oh, in those smart clubs in the thirties, they loved the sentimental
songs. And all the great songwriters were turning out beautiful
songs, every week. You took them all for granted. ADELAIDE
HALL

You couldn't write songs like Cole Porter today – our society is
freer. People aren't 'in love', like they used to be and needing songs
to say it for them. ROSETTA REITZ

A lot of the great songs came from shows, and were meant to be
listened to, in a theatre. Some came from films. And some, like
some of Billie Holiday's songs, were written for record dates. PAT
SMYTHE

When a hit came out, the whole world played it. When 'Stardust'
came out, everybody had their own idea of how 'Stardust' should
go. The old songs seem to give you more to work on, more foun-
dation. ROSE MURPHY

You could hear a song and buy a song copy. People bought the
music, not records to learn the songs. Nowadays, if you ever see a
piece of pop music written down, it's not at all like the record,
because of the studio production. NORMA WINSTONE

We find the standard songs we did maybe twenty, thirty years ago,
are very attractive to the audience. So, if we can make them
unusual, unique in the way we *do* them, we can please ourselves
too. Like, 'Hey, there's "I Got Rhythm", done *this* way – check this
out.' At the same time, they know they're hearing 'I Got Rhythm'
and they love it. ROY KRAL

★

I think songs are vehicles for singers. And vehicles for musicians. JOHNNY M

I think, to keep the excitement, one has to improvise. I used to sing
pretty strictly on the melody as I'd learnt it, because I'm not a
trained musician, so I don't *see* the chords in my mind. But, gradually, it was a matter of learning that you can extend a tune. And then
one night, you sing a phrase which *works* that you never sung
before. GEORGE MELLY

98

When I first started singing I was working in piano bar things. And I would do songs I didn't like because they were so requested. I was always into experimenting and trying things and doing things differently all the time to keep myself interested. Like 'Feelings' – I would do it up-tempo, like a fast samba. And people would say, 'How *can* you?' I was accused of doing some really flagrant things with songs.　BOBBY McFERRIN

I think it used to bother musicians that I didn't sing the melody. But I think you should do a tune the way you *feel*. Because it's been *done* straight for the last fifty years. And there's ten thousand singers out there who will sing it straight, who *can't* improvise, who don't even know how. There are extremes, sure, you can overdo it. I might be guilty of overdoing it sometimes, with carrying a tune *out* too much. But my audience is a young audience. They don't know the tune in the first place.　BETTY CARTER

My process is learning to discard things. Learning what *not* to do, what to eliminate. To get down to the essence of the song.　BOBBY COLE

As one becomes mature as a performer, editing is the game. Because you're trying everything when you're young. Just throw it all up against the wall, and anything that sticks, you keep.　ROSEMARY CLOONEY

When I first started singing, silence frightened the life out of me. I had to fill every moment. Then I listened to Peggy Lee a lot and I noted that she's very sparse – her phrasing is lovely, very open. ELAINE DELMAR

There are a million ways to do one of the great popular songs.　GEORGE SHEARING

And I think a strong song can stand up to anything.　RICHARD RODNEY BENNETT

There are two sorts of singers – the interpretative sort and the improvising sort. There are people like Sheila Jordan and Betty Carter, who wouldn't be caught dead singing the tune but start off improvising right away – sometimes it's a guessing game just what tune they *are* singing. And then there are the singers with jazz inflections who give meaning to the lyric.　PAT SMYTHE

All right, there are people who are more recognizably jazz-inspired, like Betty Carter or Norma Winstone – people who have a very strong instrumental connection, if you like. They tend to assume the rôle of an instrument. Which, to me, is a quite different exercise from song interpretation. I mean, there's that story that Cole Porter rang up Sinatra and said, 'If you hate my songs so much, why do you sing them?' Because Sinatra had changed the tempo, the phrasing, that kind of thing.   DIGBY FAIRWEATHER

The very first casting, as it were, of the tune is up to the composer. He has the power to say who should do it. But once it's been recorded, then anyone can do it. And the interpretation is up to the individual.   BOB DOROUGH

Stephen Sondheim doesn't like anyone to do anything to his songs. He expects them to be performed, with the original accompaniment, like German *lieder*. And that's why very few of his songs ever get away from the shows.   RICHARD RODNEY BENNETT

Richard Rodgers once compelled me to re-record a whole number because one note was almost the written note, and it was a new Broadway show. He was powerful enough to do this. And, in those days, you couldn't go back and just fix the single note.   MILT GABLER

In America, the great jazz musicians have always made use of popular song material.   RICHARD RODNEY BENNETT

I always reinterpret songs. Someone will say, 'That's not the right melody. You didn't sing that song *right*.' Well, pardon *me*. The composer wasn't there. And a songwriter may have a rather narrow viewpoint of his own work.   BOB DOROUGH

I think a popular song is a passport to inventiveness.   RICHARD RODNEY BENNETT

And having heard Hoagy Carmichael sing his own things, like 'Stardust' – well, it gives you the confidence to *bend* a tune.   NORMA WINSTONE

★

You've got to sing a song as though you wrote it.   RICHARD RODNEY BENNETT

It takes years sometimes to become really at one with a song. Playing and singing is great, because you can become more readily at one with a song. You wear it like a coat.   BOBBY COLE

Sometimes I get a tune I don't like at all and then I'll find myself, oh, anything from five to ten years later, singing it. As we grow older and as we experience more in music we have different feelings. SHEILA JORDAN

There are certain tunes you just have to live with. And that's what you start doing. You start singing them, and trying them on for size and getting comfortable with them and then really experiencing them.   MARILYN MOORE

I *feel* something different each time I sing a song. And I can sing a song a hundred times, but each time there'll be a little difference somewhere.   CARRIE SMITH

The point for me is to be able to sing a song in such a way that the listener believes that you personally have had the experience. In other words, you're so *convincing* with that song. I think a good singer *becomes* what he is singing about at that moment – each song is a little play. But of course you'd kill yourself if you were *really* torn up twenty times a night.   RAY CHARLES

I like to feel like a storyteller when I sing. And I have to believe the story myself, before I can tell it with any conviction.   SHEILA JORDAN

I sing about a lot of things that never happened to me. That I can just imagine.   SHIRLEY HORN

I find you match up feelings you have felt with the feelings in the song, even if they are not the same. Like, 'Lush Life' – I've never been an alcoholic, but I've certainly been as low as an alcoholic feels, and that's the feeling I go for. The songs may not be in the language I speak daily – after all, many of them are in the words of the thirties, forties, right? But I can deal with the feeling in them.   JAY CLAYTON

Are you a lover? Do you love *love*, love to be in love? Are you thinking about a particular person when you sing? That has a lot to do with how you interpret a love song. So you're telling people what it was *like*.   SHIRLEY HORN

What you are singing is the *memory* of feelings.   JACKIE CAIN

Sometimes my own feelings become too strong for the song. I sang a song called 'Love Me by Name', and I was feeling really lonely at the time – no man about, you know – and I really got into it. And I was embarrassed at the end, because I was shaking, my whole body was quivering. And the audience was looking at me and it was really quite a shock to know that I'd *really* revealed that much about myself. And it used to affect me the same almost every night. Then, all of a sudden, you *lose* that emotional thing. I don't suppose if I sang it now it would affect me the same way. It's sad when you get into a sort of *mechanical* thing – that's when I like to drop the song.   JULIE AMIET

Some songs are moving just in the *notes* of them.   SHIRLEY HORN

Sometimes the people you're playing with are so good. And they're so *with* you, they feel so much. And if you're singing a nice song, and you're half listening to them, and you're singing beautiful words, sad words of songs, everything at the same time makes it very emotional. Yes, I end up with the old tears.   BETTY SMITH

Yes, I've had to stop and take control. What does it? – a certain poignancy, a certain memory . . .   BOBBY SHORT

We feel, I guess, it's nicer to bring people up, than to bring them down. Most of the things we do together, which we're most known for, are lighthearted. Within the context of our sets, it's hard to do a very *down* thing, because people get depressed.   JACKIE CAIN

I guess I've sung the occasional sad song. Most of the time it's jollity. I don't think I'd know how to – bare my soul. I'm just a naturally jolly person, I think, who sees the funny side of life.   RAY ELLINGTON

I might have sung a few torchy tunes, but I've never been that tragic. Look, some people suffer loud, some people suffer soft.   MAXINE SULLIVAN

I sing the same songs different now – you can hear I've *been* there.   SHEILA JORDAN

Some singers choose songs that are out of key with each other, I mean it's contradictory. Like saying, 'Oh, I've lost my lover' one minute and the next, 'Oh, I'm so happy'. I think some singers are unconvincing in conveying truthful feelings because of this.   MAL WALDRON

I sing all kinds of songs, because that's life, isn't it?   SALENA JONES

I absolutely fall in love with some songs, I just cannot give them up.   CAROL KIDD

Certain tunes are so *faithful*. Even on an off night, no matter how I feel, I can always get *into* those tunes.   JAY CLAYTON

Sometimes I sing a song for a while and I get really sick of it and I won't sing it for ages. And then, when I pick it up again, it's changed. It's different. And it's like a new song for me again.   JULIE AMIET

★

Did you ever have that thing, when you listen to a singer, and you don't know what the song was *about*?   JAY CLAYTON

I heard Mabel Mercer say years ago, 'The music is in the *words* not the notes.'   CHARLES COCHRAN

The words, to me, are ninety-nine and eight-tenths of what a song is all about. If the melody is great, that's lovely, but that's just the frosting. The words are the cake.   MEL TORME

In the nice, small supper clubs I play in the States, people like sophisticated music, Cole Porter, that sort of thing. They really hang on every word. If there is a witty rhyme, they laugh aloud at it.   SUSANNAH McCORKLE

I pick songs because of the lyrics. Even when I'm playing a ballad on the saxophone I really play the words. Do you know what I mean? The *mood* of the song.   BETTY SMITH

Musicians who explore the melody with great tenderness know what the song is saying. They're the ones who know the lyric.   ROY KRAL

I feel too much emphasis is put on words. Even when I sing them, I don't get into the words too much, you know.   CHET BAKER

I sing the lyrics with my horn.   LESTER YOUNG

Musicians often don't listen to the words even when the singer is singing them.   JACKIE CAIN

I think words are often put over better by piano bar singers who generally aren't all the way into jazz. They really are dedicated to the lyrics.   RICHARD RODNEY BENNETT

I like to sing the words as if I was talking to someone.   SHIRLEY HORN

To be as direct as you'd be to a good friend in conversation – that's what I've always loved about Billie Holiday and the greatest lesson I've learned from her.   SUSANNAH McCORKLE

I know that if I don't feel I understand completely what a lyric *is* I find it hard to convey to the audience.   CLEO LAINE

I had my political consciousness raised in the sixties, through working with Archie Shepp. Before that, I just sang the songs. Now, if I'm singing a standard, I make it *work*. Like, 'I'll Remember April' – I'll pick out the word 'remember', because if you remember, you remember who you are and you will remember your history and people tend to forget fast. A message to the blacks is remembrance.   JOE LEE WILSON

I don't care how beautiful, how witty or how extraordinary the lyrics are, if it doesn't mean anything to *me*.   SHEILA JORDAN

When I first started singing standards I had a lot of trouble with the words. I thought they were trite. Particularly ballads. I was young then, and I would do up-tempo things, and I would learn the words, but I was using the words as vehicles, as articulation.   JAY CLAYTON

There are always words, even in the best songs, that are silly. If you're a feminist, it must be hard.   CLEO LAINE

There must be hundreds of old songs that must cause women *intense* annoyance.   DIGBY FAIRWEATHER

There was a whole school of those torch songs, wasn't there? That whole masochistic torch song thing – songs like 'My Man' and 'Moanin' Low'. I used to sing 'Good for Nothing Joe', and when you look at the lyrics – 'He beats the hell out of me', all that – these days it's insulting women to sing them.   ANNIE ROSS

What annoys me is when they just *mouth* these words, as if they don't really know what it's like to fucking go *through* those experiences. That makes me feel really uncomfortable and demeaned as a woman, because they're just taking them for granted. But someone can sing them as if it's a way of exorcizing what they're going through, and make it as beautiful as possible through music – do you know what I mean? I'm not saying this to glamourize it or glorify it, because I can't sing those songs now. But, because of who I was then, I could sing them. How I've changed has changed the sort of words I can sing. I have to sing about how I feel as a woman now, today. Because I *was* a terrible masochist in lots of ways, but I didn't

104

realize it. I thought it was love and romance or whatever.   MAGGIE
NICOLS

You're going to sing 'Misty' like it *meant* something? Nobody but an
idiot is going to believe those lyrics and try to sing them as if they
meant something. It's a *mood*: you can't get meaning out of it,
there's nothing there to *express*. It's a perfect lyric because it estab-
lishes a mood – something you don't have to think about. But for a
singer to get up there and sing it meaningfully, with gestures, and try
to put some kind of heartfelt emotion into 'I get misty whenever
you're near' is ludicrous. Or, if this indeed is how she really feels, is
it her *job* as a singer to tell us how she feels? Or is it her job to
present us a song? Are we in this for self-expression, or for musical
expression?   DAVE FRISHBERG

If it's a song that's not in your generation – I mean, like 'Sophisticated Lady' – there's a way to do it – you may have to do a little
tongue-in-cheek thing. But you emphasize, you don't de-emphasize
the words, the ideas. And you find musical ideas, phrases, come out
of the words, too.   JAY CLAYTON

You can sometimes put a thought in, sort of, inverted commas, you
know. So the audience knows that you know the words are a bit –
corny.   ELAINE DELMAR

There's moving stories, there's funny stories, lighthearted things,
cute things, some witty ditties, you know. But when you sing them,
you're supposed to *say* something.   BETTY CARTER

A lot of people say that Ella Fitzgerald doesn't sing a lyric with
meaning, that she doesn't understand what she's singing. Yet, when
I listen to her sing that song book series – you know those records? –
these to me are the definitive versions. Maybe it's because she
doesn't attempt to imbue each line with special meanings and
everything, she's just treating it as a musical phrase to be sung in a
musical and economical way. The *song* comes right across.   DAVE
FRISHBERG

In fact, people don't seem to listen to the words these days, it's
hardly fashionable, just to the general effect of the group, of the
whole thing.   PAT SMYTHE

I don't think there's much *left* in the word-value of a lot of jazz
standards. Let's just take, 'Our Love is Here to Stay'. It's a good
lyric, but are we really engaged in the line 'Gibraltar may tumble'?

We just don't even *see* those images any more.   DAVE FRISHBERG

I sing in English to audiences all over the world who don't understand English. And yet I'm able to touch them in some way. I think it's the manner in which sounds are made. It can be very expressive, the emotional content of the sound.   HELEN MERRILL

Sometimes just hearing the sound of the words is nice.   NORMA WINSTONE

My husband was a sound poet, and that showed me another way of dealing with word *sounds*, not scatting you know, but taking the word apart. And I worked that way for about three years.   JEANNE LEE

I've been accused sometimes of not really thinking what songs are about. Because I've always been into the sounds of words, rather than the words themselves.   BOBBY McFERRIN

★

Once you start singing jazz songs which were originally instrumentals it's hard. The average pop song is written with the limitations of the average pop singer in mind. And it's hard if you sing words fitted to instrumental solos. But when I'm teaching, I say, 'It's as easy as it is hard.' People are inhibited by things they don't need to be inhibited by.   JOE LEE WILSON

People are writing words to all kinds of classic jazz instrumentals. But just having words is not enough. They've got to be *good* words, not just a word for each note of the tune.   JAY CLAYTON

I've been trying to write words for some of the things John writes for our group Azimuth. It's very difficult to find the right words. You can have words that sound good but don't mean anything much. But I try to find some meaning through the whole piece, words that sound good next to each other, but when you read them appear to have a meaning.   NORMA WINSTONE

I've written lyrics to some Bird lines. There's a lot of notes, so they're very fast and very *wordy*.   SHEILA JORDAN

What inspired my words to 'Twisted'? It's called *money*. I just listened to the Wardell Gray record and I remember thinking what 'Twisted' meant to *me*, and I tried to give it a beginning, a middle and an end – a story.   ANNIE ROSS

There's a lot of work in putting words to instrumental solos. Takes

106

an artist who's pretty fast to do that. I never heard anybody like Jon Hendricks, he's *fast*. He's got a fast musical mind.   SLIM GAILLARD

Jon is a genius. I think he's the best bebop lyricist living today. He can make words to your solo *while* you're playing it. And you don't remember your solo *yourself*. You come off the stand and he has words for it.   JOE LEE WILSON

Putting words to solos is Jon's forte. It's a fun thing.   JOE WILLIAMS

I make my living with words. Words may be an imperfect vehicle for expressing our ideas, but they're the best we have.   JON HENDRICKS

We worked together for about eight months. And I love him so much I named my son after him.   BOBBY McFERRIN

I think Eddie Jefferson did it first. He did the words to the 'I'm in the Mood for Love' solo I made in 1949.   JAMES MOODY

Eddie was a dear friend and a witty man. He basically was a tap dancer. And he started writing lyrics to musicians' solos. I remember, he said when Charlie Parker came along, it really made it hard for him.   JOE LEE WILSON

Eddie was involved with me and my bands for almost twenty years. I regarded him as my friend and as the singer with the group. You know, when you hear music you hear something – sometimes you might hear a story. And that's what Eddie did. He heard a story in the music.   JAMES MOODY

Eddie said that when he came to New York Babs Gonzales was writing already. Babs' group did all original compositions.   JOE LEE WILSON

I had been watching Billy Eckstine and I began to realize that to make long bread one had to be a singer and look pretty for the girls. In May of 1946, I started rehearsing my first group, Babs, Three Bips and a Bop.   BABS GONZALES

I was very attracted by the hip lyrics that came out of the bebop singers.   JOE LEE WILSON

Early in 1947 we cut our first date. The tunes were 'Oop Pop A Da', 'Pay Dem Dues' 'Lop Pow' and 'Weird Lullaby'. Charlie Ventura was the first to emulate our style and in two months of constant plugging he became the 'Originator of the "Bop" Vocals'.   BABS GONZALES

King Pleasure – well, he was a strange kind of guy, you know. Mad? I don't know . . .   JOE LEE WILSON

King Pleasure is a jazz musician who plays tonsils. King Pleasure is his name and jazz singing is his game, and what he sings is right because it's what he wrote, and what he wrote is right because right is the only way he ever wrote, unquote.   JON HENDRICKS

He always had this feeling that somebody was going to take something from him. He said he had an invention that he wanted to patent, and he was always afraid someone was going to steal it from him. The invention? How you could live for ever.   JOE LEE WILSON

Joe Carroll, he made it his business doing scat and all that with Dizzy's band. He's dead now. I saw Babs a couple of days before he died in the hospital. Then I played with Joe Carroll – we did a thing up in the mountains and a month or so later he was dead. He wasn't ill, he just had a heart attack – bam! Dave Lambert, who was in it right from the beginning, car crash. King Pleasure just passed. And Eddie – well, I never really knew what happened.   JAMES MOODY

My hero, Eddie Jefferson, was just getting his own *back*, when that nut shot the gun – and, you know, the murderer is out walking the streets in Detroit again. They got him off on a technicality.   MARK MURPHY

★

People used to say that an audience has to understand the words, but more and more I think that words are good when they can be explicit, but when they cannot, words can become sounds. You are better off putting your emotion into humming the song than saying words to it.   FLORA PURIM

If you sing something without words, it can mean whatever the listener wants it to mean.   NORMA WINSTONE

I didn't sing words when I was embarrassed about my English accent and having to make those words got in the way of the music.   FLORA PURIM

Improvisation in a singer disturbs a lot of people.   MARK MURPHY

I was working with Michael Garrick at a girls' school and when I did my improvisation, a row of them went into *hysterics* right in front of me. They didn't laugh when I sang words. They didn't laugh at the instrumentals.   NORMA WINSTONE

People are used to songs being an unchanging line of storytelling. Singers have always been the storytellers. Then a jazz singer is not only singing words, but improvising without words, or doing it different each time. It makes an audience work hard.   MARK MURPHY

Look, when you've sung the song, just take it out, finish with it. Unless you feel like screaming around, what they call scat singing. JIMMY ROWLES

Is this singer trying to impress me with his voice, his technique, his jazz savvy? I'm not interested in some guy trying to sing like a horn, or some woman trying to imitate Charlie Parker.   DAVE FRISHBERG

What can the voice do? Either it sings words or it imitates instruments.   BOB DOROUGH

I was intrigued by the bebop singers, I thought it was funny. And it is. They were entertainers, of course; I don't think any of them said, 'Listen to how *creative* I am.' But to try and pass that off as some kind of profound jazz expression doesn't cut any ice with me. Because there are more direct and easy and effective ways of doing that. Like, play the tenor sax.   DAVE FRISHBERG

Saying I'm a frustrated tenor player negates an old and noble art form – scat singing.   JON HENDRICKS

I find it very insulting to be called an instrumental *impersonator*. Because I feel I am an instrument.   BOBBY McFERRIN

The question is, do they really improvise? Or do they fall back on licks they know or can remember hearing instrumentalists do? ROY KRAL

I wouldn't even call it jazz. I would call it someone trying to copy jazz.   MILT GABLER

Most singers would be smarter to step to one side and let the instrumentalists take it over, before they start hitting the sixth about eight thousand times.   ROY KRAL

If you're going to scat, you better be able to play as good as any of the jazz musicians, that's all. You better be able to improvise as well as they do. The best scat singers have always been musicians – Clark Terry, Dizzy, James Moody . . .   HELEN MERRILL

It was James Moody who started me on that. He'd sit down and say, 'What is this song?' and leave out the melody line. So it tuned my ear for chords. He taught me to *listen*.   ANNIE ROSS

A musician will pick the right notes. Whereas a person who didn't know music would not.   JAMES MOODY

Scatting is more of a challenge, really, than playing.   CHET BAKER

It's more difficult to sing a jazz solo than play a jazz solo. Because you've got no notes to press down. You've got to find those notes and make those notes.   BETTY SMITH

It all arose because everyone wanted to do bebop music. Singers too. And there weren't words enough for it. And singing all the bebop changes is the most fun, it's a challenge.   SHEILA JORDAN

The music was so exciting, everyone wanted to do it. And singers wanted to extend the whole business of singing a song.   ANNIE ROSS

I'd never tried to do it, the saxophone did it for me. And then one day somebody says, 'Oh, listen, it goes . . .' and scatted, like you would hum a Charlie Parker solo – and that's how people used to do it. It was because a whole generation was learning Charlie Parker solos off the records.   JAMES MOODY

It was Bird made you want to do it.   SHEILA JORDAN

It's no big mysterious thing. What Diz was doing with non-words was very different from what Louis Armstrong or Roy Eldridge was doing – though people have been doing it since the twenties. I remember, I used to hear people do 'Spodeeodoh deeoh spodeeo-doh', things like that. Then, with Dizzy, it's 'Ooh oodeeoocoo coo coo oodle ee oh'. And some say, 'Oodle dee doodle ee oh', but that 'Dee doodle dee doo doo' has to get in there, 'Be doodle de bap bap' you know.   JAMES MOODY

It was funny sounds, ear-catching, what Dizzy Gillespie did when bebop came in, and they swung and were humorous and crazy and all that. But it all goes back to the twenties and people like Red McKenzie.   MILT GABLER

They say scat singing was born when Louis Armstrong forgot the lyrics and – you have to sing something – so he starts singing sounds, nonsense.   BOB DOROUGH

110

I was standing in the wings, must have been about 1927, listening to Duke Ellington. I closed the first half of the show, and when Duke was playing I went down to listen. And I listened to all these gorgeous tunes. And I heard this melody and I was singing this little counter-melody while he was playing. And he said, 'That was lovely, it's what I want, do it again.' And I said, 'I don't know what I did.' And he said, 'Try it.' And he had this recording session. And I was scared, but we did it. I don't think he did wordless instrumental vocal things again until the forties.   ADELAIDE HALL

Did you know Bon Bon, who sang with Jan Savitt's band in the thirties? He was a slightly better structured scat singer than was Cab Calloway. It was like singing band phrases, not truly improvisational perhaps, but it was super.   MEL TORME

Leo Watson – he had a group called the Five Spirits of Rhythm on 52nd Street – he improvised. He would imitate instruments, like a trombone. He was a funny man. The Mills Brothers did that first, and the Boswell girls, imitating instruments.   MILT GABLER

Leo Watson, he was the best, oh, the best, the best scat singer that ever did it.   PETER DEAN

Leo Watson is the first and only guy I ever heard of whom I could say, 'That was a jazz singer.' For a man, and that includes me, he was the best scat singer I ever heard.   MEL TORME

He worked with me, recorded with me. He was original. Everybody in Hollywood used to come in and listen to him. And they'd follow everything he said, because he could sing about anything. He'd start singing about the walls, the rug, tables, ashtray, he'd just sing. Yes, I guess he was way up in the skies somewhere. I was the square of the group because I stuck to my malted milk shake.   SLIM GAILLARD

Listen to Leo on Gene Krupa's record of 'Nagasaki', that's what scat singing is all about.   MEL TORME

His records have just disappeared.   PETER DEAN

Leo Watson was the creator, everybody followed him.   SLIM GAILLARD

We'd meet in the elevator, and he'd say, 'Are you ready, man?' and I'd say, 'Sure.' And he'd go, 'Zip de deedle doop de oo' and we'd do four bars apiece, back and forth. He really was one of my inspirations.   PETER DEAN

The truth of the matter is that scat singing is the toughest kind of singing. There's very few people that can sing scat. There's me and Ella and Sarah and Carmen. And that's really it.   MEL TORME

Ella was the first of the girls – no, Ann Robinson, a girl who sang on 52nd Street was the first I heard. She really copied Leo Watson. She was terrific. And she died when she was young.   MILT GABLER

And Betty Roche, that 'Take the "A" Train' of hers, was one of the first scat things I heard.   JULIA STEELE

When I recorded Ella's first scat things, 'Lady Be Good' and 'How High the Moon', tape had just started to come in. And we would tape her version of it, and have the arranger write stuff behind her, and she would improvise jazz licks in her interpretation of the tune – it's her memory for jazz improvisations, her pitching and the way she swings.   MILT GABLER

Anita O'Day is good at it – it's swing improvising. Mel Torme scats very well, but his is a little more stylized, than, say, Betty Carter's. I think she really does do just what she feels at the moment.   SHEILA JORDAN

No one can do what Mel does. He's such a good musician, he knows exactly how to structure his phrases, and, when he scats, though it's improvised, he always knows where he's going in the music.   PETER DEAN

I do 'Route Sixty-Six' every night. It is never the same. There are some quotes, identifiable quotes that I throw in purposely, for the uninitiated.   MEL TORME

I do it because it was the first way I learned to do jazz. I was scat singing before I used words. And I was going to do my own sound in scat singing, whether it was accepted or not. It's an emotional feeling – and it's an emotional sound. I have this little thing of my own, and it comes to me and I hear it and I sing it. Some people say it's insane and wonderful. And other people say it's dreadful. You don't have to like it, but it's unique. I haven't stolen it from anybody else.   SHEILA JORDAN

Scat is the least limited form of singing there is to do. Because, if you can come up with the ideas, you can sing the blues or a thirty-two-bar form, like 'Lady Be Good' *forever.*   MEL TORME

In 1939 I went to work in this club in Chicago. I was the house singer. I had twenty-four minutes to fill and very few tunes to fill that time with – five numbers. On the tunes I knew I could do five or six different versions of the chorus; I'd begin with the melody and end with the melody and what went on in between depended on what hit me while I was up there singing .ᵃ. . I saved 'Lady Be Good' as an encore. At the point where the bridge comes to the second chorus, I needed an idea from somewhere. I saw a polka-dot blouse. So I developed that chorus as a bagful of polka-dots. To keep the version going, I searched for new ideas. Where was I going to get my inspiration? I looked around the room and that gave me the idea of singing the structure of the room – long wall, short wall, long wall, short wall. That gave me the frame for that chorus. I turned to the band. Five men. So I put it into a five rhythm. Anything that I could get an idea from I put to work to fill out my time on the stand . . . In all I did twelve choruses of 'Lady Be Good' and when I finished the place exploded.   ANITA O'DAY

She's a totally honest lady, but if Anita tells you a story, it's about as close to the truth as she is to the melody when she sings.   CHARLES COCHRAN

The music is really going by pretty fast, you know. You really don't have much chance to think, 'What will I do here?' You just do it. It's the way musicians think when they play. I don't have, like, a saxophone in my head, or a trumpet. I'm not thinking, oh, I'm going to compete with this musician and outblow him, that's not what I'm thinking about.   BETTY CARTER

A lot of things can go wrong. The tempo can be too fast. Or you're not grooving with the changes. Or you're not grooving with everybody else.   SHEILA JORDAN

You hear a chord and you hear all the intervals. And then you pick one note that no one expects and sing it.   FLORA PURIM

You can always tell when someone is thinking, 'Oh, I don't want to hit a wrong note, so I've got it all smoothed out and polished, so let's not take chances.' I'd rather hit some wrong notes.   SHEILA JORDAN

Mind you, I think a little scat goes a long way. I think Ella is the greatest, and she very wisely limits her scat choruses to just enough.   MEL TORME

The only thing I find a bit distracting is that, whereas a musician has his own abstract sound, a singer has to use some form of vocal syllables – what we call 'shoobeedoo-ing'.   DIGBY FAIRWEATHER

I don't use any syllables when I scat, I just try to make a sound. You just make a sound, but very softly right in the mike and it comes out like an instrument.   CHET BAKER

You have to invent your own syllables. And that's beautiful because it's a part of expressing you. There's no standard way to do that. There's no standard way to do *jazz*, either.   SAL MOSCA

I say, 'Don't do those other singers' things. Don't learn their solos, their syllables. That's not *true*.' I think some people are scatting too soon – before they understand the song.   JAY CLAYTON

I like scat singing the way it's being done in New York at the moment. Singers like Jay Clayton, and Sheila with her roots in bebop, and Jeanne Lee, who's a good improviser.   MAL WALDRON

I learned my sound doubling unisons with horns; you have to learn how to make a certain instrumental sound or you will stand out. I've been in quintets and sextets like that, and I love it. And I swear people think I'm another horn, because I'm blending.   JAY CLAYTON

I would *rather* spend my time singing without words. I'm really into vocal music.   BOBBY McFERRIN

It's a time now when singers want to scat. And it's people like me who are doing it to them. They hear some of this new stuff that we're doing, and it's personal, and it can be exciting to a singer who hears it, and they say, 'I'd like to do that.' But they can't *start* there. I was lucky enough to have all those free-jazz sessions in the early sixties. And when I had to guts to do it, I would open my mouth and I would accompany sounds.   JAY CLAYTON

As far as I'm concerned, there's only one woman who's doing what jazz singing should be. And that's Urszula Dudziak. For me, she combines everything as a jazz singer. Nothing to do with the songs, or the cabaret, or to do with the emotion – it's pure jazz singing as an instrument.   PEPI LEMER

I found that you can reach people without words. That is my passion now. And I'm completely involved in it.   URSZULA DUDZIAK

I am the first instrument. I am the voice. I do not imitate other instruments. Other instruments imitate *me*.   ABBEY LINCOLN

6
What With?

. . . they talk about voices. And the business of passing
on what they know about singing jazz . . .

I've grown accustomed to my voice.   CHARLES COCHRAN

I *love* my voice, are you kidding? I'm my own best critic.   JOE LEE
WILSON

Jesus, I've been working for forty years to improve it, to make it
sound better to me.   JOE WILLIAMS

I enjoy singing. I never particularly enjoyed hearing myself
sing.   MOSE ALLISON

I have a wispy, head-toney quality. I'd like a more robust
sound.   MEL TORME

My ears are better than my chops.   HELEN MERRILL

There was a time when I was very leery of singing, because I had all
kinds of hang-ups about singing. Much as I wanted to sing. The
reason I didn't sing was that I was afraid of it. Because I felt that I
didn't sing well. That I couldn't sustain notes. That I didn't have any
range. That I sang out of tune. That I didn't have any voice. Oh, I
had every neurotic hang-up about singing that one could have. And
I always compared myself to the singers I admired and I always
came out second best. Instead of *doing* it, I was doing it and
listening to it. And commenting. And criticizing. Now I just *do*
it.   BARBARA CARROLL

117

The great instrumentalists, like Nat Cole, Louis Armstrong, Jack Teagarden, Woody Herman, even, are interesting singers because the *music* comes first, not the 'great voice' ego trip. The music is the whole thing. And the voice makes sense because it *is* the music.   RAY CHARLES

A lot of the great people didn't have great voices. Well, Louis Armstrong didn't have a great voice, did he? But his singing was a knock-out, because it was just all jazz.   BETTY SMITH

Jazz musicians often manage to be very good singers, which must be annoying to trained popular singers. The last thing you need to be a singer in jazz is a *voice*. But you certainly need everything else.   DIGBY FAIRWEATHER

My singing? When I first did it a lot of them liked it and a lot of them hated it. I know that, from not even being in the polls, ever, as a singer. I tied Nat Cole for third place in 1954 on the strength of my first album.   CHET BAKER

A voice is not very important to the interpretation of songs. I think Walter Huston proved that with 'September Song'.   SYLVIA SYMS

If you work with jazz musicians it's the expressiveness of the vocal equipment that is the most important.   ANNIE ROSS

How you sing is not nearly as important as how you sing *what* you sing.   SYLVIA SYMS

I'd much rather listen to other people than myself.   GEORGE MELLY

I never think of my voice at all. I just know the kind of feeling I'm getting from what I'm singing about.   SHEILA JORDAN

I've been compared to a saxophone with asthma.   BOB DOROUGH

Most jazz singers – Eddie Jefferson, King Pleasure, Jon Hendricks for example – don't have big voices. They have pleasant voices and a style. But they don't use the voice as power. To me, it's a business, my voice. Voice Incorporated.   JOE LEE WILSON

Some of my favourite singers are the people with no voices. You know what I'm talking about, don't you?   BARBARA CARROLL

I find a perfect voice gets in the way in jazz.   RICHARD RODNEY BENNETT

I have a *sound*. I don't have a voice, like a *voice*, like Sarah Vaughan's voice. She has a *voice*, I don't have that. Billie Holiday had a sound. Not a voice.   BETTY CARTER

Many great singers have self-made voices. It's as if the wish to communicate in music overcomes the lack. You get the occasional extraordinarily beautiful voice like Sarah and Cleo, Sandra King, Mel Torme. But then you get people like Anita O'Day, who don't have great voices, but somehow it moves me more. And certainly, in many ways, Billie Holiday got more moving as her vocal equipment faded.   RICHARD RODNEY BENNETT

I've always had this *nothing* voice, it's a microphone voice. Not everybody dug it. One of the critics said, 'Anita O'Day should clear her throat.'   ANITA O'DAY

Singers tend to get hung up on their golden tones, too.   RICHARD RODNEY BENNETT

I've noticed some nights, when I'm really warmed up, I may do a little listening to my voice. And then I notice that no one *else* is listening to me.   CHARLES COCHRAN

It's like looking in a mirror. I'm not in love with my own face, and I'm not in love with my own voice.   SUSANNAH McCORKLE

If you're singing a song with lyrics, that's when the voice comes into play because it's the tone of it that makes the thing work. But scatting is another art form altogether. Like, with Sarah Vaughan singing a ballad, the voice is *there*. But when it comes to scatting, improvising, her voice has a tendency to get in the way, because it's just too *voice*. It doesn't sound raw, like an instrument.   BETTY CARTER

Yes, you might say I *make* my voice out of the feelings which make it do more than it might do naturally.   RAY CHARLES

I think I have a wonderful *instrument*. It will accommodate itself to anything I want to sing. This didn't just happen. In order for it to emerge, it's been forged and wrought and shaped over the years.   ABBEY LINCOLN

I've asked my voice to do different things, and that's how it's grown. When you first heard me with Chick Corea, I was still learning his songs. He liked us to duplicate his melodies and sing in the original keys. He wouldn't change the keys to make it easier for me, and thanks to him, I stretched my octaves.   FLORA PURIM

I don't think about my voice very much unless I'm asked. I would like to change it. I *did* change it. I had only an octave and a half when I started. Now, with what I know of microphone techniques, I have four and a half octaves on records and in performance. John thinks I can do anything he can write. I say, 'I can't do that.' He says, 'Well, don't just dismiss it. Go away and have a go.' Sometimes I go away in a huff and work and work and I come back just to show him that it *cannot* be done. And I find I've found a way it *can* be done.   CLEO LAINE

I hit one note on 'Avenue C' and someone said to Dave Lambert, 'What's that note Annie hits?' And he said, 'I don't want to tell her. Because if she knew, she might not be able to hit it.'   ANNIE ROSS

If you're a creative jazz singer, when you can't hit a high note, you hit a low note. But it's the *right* note.   BOB DOROUGH

Your voice should do what you want it to do. It's a muscle, and it responds to stimulus, and it responds to your mind.   LEON THOMAS

I think my voice is starting to do more easily what I feel. For a long time I could *not* listen to it.   JAY CLAYTON

I think singing is ninety per cent in your head.   ANNIE ROSS

It has a lot to do with your confidence. And your age. I mean, they tell me a voice doesn't mean much before your early thirties. But for the first fifteen years or so, there was always that question – will it be there the way I want it? Will I have enough breath? All that stuff.   JAY CLAYTON

I think you feel different ways about your voice at different times of your life. I think when I started I just always took it for granted.   ROSEMARY CLOONEY

I didn't burn my voice out early. I started later than most and over the years the voice has built up to quite a lot of strength. And all this . . . fame has come to me at an age when most people think, oh I'm finished. How long it will remain up there depends on how healthy I keep. My throat man says you can go on singing *ad infinitum* as long as you're healthy.   CLEO LAINE

People tell me all the time, 'You sound just like you did twenty years ago.' But to me, my sound varies from night to night. That's the challenge every night: trying to work towards that spot where it's all *flowing*. Sometimes it comes easy, sometimes it comes hard, sometimes it doesn't come at all.   MOSE ALLISON

You've got two or three voices. I've got a road voice and a home voice. And something in between. On a gig, if *this* voice doesn't work, I make another one down *here*. Almost every trick in the book comes into it. Because some nights you're forced to use them.   MARK MURPHY

When I did cabaret, I lost all emotional quality in my voice. I was afraid, and my voice sounded like that – hard and tense. I drank a lot. And my voice became very hard. But I'd become a very hard person.   JULIE AMIET

As I worked and became more secure with what I was doing, my voice changed a lot. Also, all my life experiences have made me stronger. So I *speak* stronger when I sing now. I can even speak low, and people will listen to me.   FLORA PURIM

★

Sylvia Syms – she really is the best nowadays in terms of lady singers singing popular songs – she told me she does her best singing when she has a bad throat, so she has to put the voice aside and get into the other qualities, the meaning of the words, the unheard, the unseen.   CHARLES COCHRAN

You learn to sing *round* a sore throat.   LEON THOMAS

I sang with a cold and I could only hold notes for a fraction of the time I usually liked to. But the interesting thing was, I had a hoarse quality in my voice, that made it sadder. And it made some numbers much stronger. Because I tend to think my voice is a bit sweet. Sometimes when you're not in full voice, you have a more moving sound.   SUSANNAH McCORKLE

I used to get very hoarse, and people used to say, 'It's lovely, hoarse.'   BERYL BRYDEN

You don't lose your musical sense, whatever may happen to your voice. You can still be interesting to listen to.   CHRIS CONNOR

You have to feel that you're going to do it, whether you can or not.   JIMMY WITHERSPOON

It's real hard work, singing with Dixieland bands like I do. All those years of no mikes and bad mikes – I suppose that's why I've got a loud voice. Probably why it's a croaky one, too.   BERYL BRYDEN

If you're working every night, the motto is, 'Don't waste it.'   JOE WILLIAMS

The thing is not to talk. That's what wastes the voice.   JOE LEE WILSON

I do my utmost to be as healthy as possible. I keep myself from too much partying, you know.   BOBBY McFERRIN

I went to a musician's party, and I said, 'I'll serve behind the bar for you', and mine host's doctor came up and said, 'What are you doing all that work for?' And I said, 'It saves me talking to people.' And he said, 'What a sensible girl you are.'   BETTY SMITH

You must get sleep. It's the only thing that helps the voice. I always try to sleep a couple of hours before a concert.   JOE LEE WILSON

You try to get early nights, because it does help the voice. But you just lie there thinking how rotten your voice is, and will it be worse in the morning?   ELAINE DELMAR

There's no rest for the weary. I learned to sing with tonsils the size of golf balls.   LEON THOMAS

Sometimes I can have been having late nights and doing things which I'd think have a bad effect, and it's fine. It's hard to say *what* causes trouble.   NORMA WINSTONE

When your professional career has been ninety per cent in night-clubs, with smoke, of course your voice is fragile.   BOBBY SHORT

There are times when my voice just dries up. And in order not to go completely paranoid, I have to do a quick head trip on myself and make a joke of it – 'Ho, ho, your voice isn't working tonight.' It's easy to get depressed. Your nerves are stripped raw up there.   MARK MURPHY

I lost my voice one time and it was a bit scary because I had to keep turning work down. I went to a Harley Street specialist. And his first words were, 'Do you smoke?' And I said, 'Yes.' And he said, 'Come back and see me when you've given it up.' And I've never smoked from that day to this.   BETTY SMITH

You can't always guarantee the mechanisms. I try never to worry too long about whether my throat is going to hold out. Because if I start dwelling on it, that's *it*.   SHEILA JORDAN

You do it, whether you can or not.   JIMMY WITHERSPOON

How do I look after my voice? Conscientiously. I smoke about forty cigarettes a day and I have about three bottles of champagne. It all helps.   RAY ELLINGTON

I just sing as much as possible. You've got all the time from the minute you wake up to the time you go to sleep.   BOBBY McFERRIN

★

An instrument is an extension of you. Whereas a voice is part of you, part of your being. I think the way you live and the way you feel about life enters into your performance.   JACKIE CAIN

The more I find out about *myself*, the more I know about my voice. The two things go together.   JULIE AMIET

You can always just lay there with what God gave you. But if you don't *know* what he gave you, and you lose it you don't know what you've lost.   BILLY ECKSTINE

One time, I asked John Hammond to find me a voice teacher, and he said, 'Oh no, Helen, I wouldn't do that for anything. Because it takes away everything you've got on your own.' There is a difference between someone that's *taught* and someone that's taught *themselves* and has their own way of doing it.   HELEN HUMES

If you take a gospel singer, for instance, and she starts studying voice, it is possible that she will lose that natural kind of vocal production that she had.   BILL DILLARD

I suppose a *produced* voice just isn't a jazz voice.   CLEO LAINE

I had a very good voice teacher, but she wasn't into any other kind of singing, so I couldn't consult her about concept or timbre, or musical line, or vibrato versus non-vibrato. And what I found out was that if I sang a jazz tune in too high a key, I could make the notes all right, but, because of the vocal training, it just didn't sound right. It wasn't the right feeling, it sounded too, quote, unquote, classical. I could sing arias that way but it wasn't what I heard in jazz. I found that the first thing was to put the key down, and, immediately, I got a more relaxed production.   JAY CLAYTON

When singers' vowels, for instance, are too produced, it gets right in my way. That's why most classical singers, even good ones, cannot sing popular songs.   RICHARD RODNEY BENNETT

A lot of singers who have learned how to sing can't forget it.   CLEO
LAINE

When I sang with Basie I had to sing Joe Williams songs in the bass
range, and Jimmy Rushing songs in the tenor range. And a voice
teacher would say I was a baritone.   LEON THOMAS

A lot of trained singers are afraid of *hurting* the voice by using the
throat. Popular singers are more reckless.   CLEO LAINE

I tell my young students, that if you keep exploring the right songs
for you and the keys, and tempos, and phrasing, eventually you'll
find the right sound for you. But you have to go through a whole
adjustment period to make this sound.   JAY CLAYTON

Every student is limited by his teacher. Because the teacher is only
teaching what he knows. And experience teaches you something
else.   LEON THOMAS

I studied trumpet when I was with Earl Hines. And then, later,
when I had my own band, I studied valve trombone. It connects up
with singing, in a way. It helps your breathing. Breathing to me is
the secret, if there is such a thing as a secret. You breathe according
to what you need, to make sense of the lyric. Like speaking.   BILLY
ECKSTINE

To hold a long note, you know what that requires? A lot of muscular
work.   JACKIE CAIN

You know Anita O'Day's fabulous breath control? She told me that
the mental process of that is to, as if you were fishing, reel the line
in, rather than casting out – think of breathing in, in, all the time,
rather than out. And it works for me.   CHARLES COCHRAN

I can hold a note any time without vibrato, I know. I became
conscious of this when I was very young. In fact, when I was married
to Aaron Sachs, who was a clarinet player, he insulted me. And he
said, 'You've got to be able to sing without vibrato.' As you know,
the bebop players were more or less vibrato-less, it was the
fashionable sound. So at a teeny age, I started to practise to do this.
It was one of the many things I learned to do by listening to
musicians.   HELEN MERRILL

I feel fortunate that I heard more instrumentalists than singers when
I started. When you learn a tune from a singer's record you usually
learn their phrasing too.   JAY CLAYTON

124

To be an imitator is important because we all have to start some-where.   SYLVIA SYMS

Clark Terry says, 'Don't worry about imitation. All of us started by imitating somebody else.'   JOE WILLIAMS

I was totally unself-conscious about copying people, accent and all, when I started. These songs are designed for a certain intonation and a certain accent. I justify it logically to myself by saying that if an English person sings Italian opera he doesn't sing it in English. I don't feel it's like . . . blacking up, I think it's crucial to doing the songs.   GEORGE MELLY

I'd listened to the great singers like Billie and Ella and Sarah and I was trying hard *not* to sing like them. I knew if I did I'd be a lost soul really.   CLEO LAINE

I worked with a teacher for a year and he wouldn't let me sing a song any way but straight. No bending notes, *nothing*. So I became conscious of, and got rid of some mannerisms I'd picked up almost without knowing.   ABBEY LINCOLN

A teacher can either say, 'Get rid of those nasty little habits.' Or you can make them into a good feature. That's really the art of being stylish, isn't it?   CLEO LAINE

The very thing that has become my trademark, a teacher would call 'excess vibrato' and try to teach out of me. I was able to do it all my life and I knew there were precedents in the calls the Pygmies make.
LEON THOMAS

Ralph Flanagan, who arranged for the Pastor band, used to say my attack on words was too harsh. And now it's probably the most recognizable thing about my singing.   ROSEMARY CLOONEY

If you study most of the singers with individuality and style, it's because they have a *flaw*, generally. And they have made the best advantage of that flaw and put it to good use. And then you get people who copy the flaw.   CLEO LAINE

I used to play piano and that's how I taught myself to sing. I get the music and I learn the song. I don't listen to no records. I don't even listen to my own.   HELEN HUMES

I encourage the singers who come to me to learn to accompany themselves on piano, even if they don't play well. Then they know what's going on.   SAL MOSCA

There were no courses in jazz when I was young. You had to hang out with the musicians and get them to show you things. SHEILA JORDAN

It was all a closely guarded secret, jazz, wasn't it? MAGGIE NICOLS

I was teaching for five years at City College, and a lot of singers wanted to sing jazz. But you can't teach anyone to sing jazz. I mean, jazz is life and you have to live it. But you can teach some of the fundamental things they should know to make their gig easier. SHEILA JORDAN

My classes are to give singers basic experience with a piano player who can play, with a sound system and occasionally with a rhythm section. And I have lots of repertoire for them to look through. It's like little steps. When they're ready I tell them to go and sit in. JAY CLAYTON

You need to be musically prepared and that takes discipline. HELEN MERRILL

Either you've got to work, or you've got to practise. If you don't, you don't move at all, except *back*. And the only way to know whether what you're practising is good or bad, is to do it on the job. BETTY CARTER

People come to music with all kinds of motives. Part of my task as a teacher is to remove all the neurotic motives that they bring to music, and to get them to enjoy music for its own sake. For instance, someone might think that music is a way to a fortune. Other people think it's a way to meet other people. Other people see it as a way out of their social status, or a way to fame, some kind of reputation in the world. All these motives are natural enough. People, our parents, the church, the schools, encourage us to compete, to succeed. But I come from the opposite place. I say that the beauty of music and your own self-development is what we're dealing with. I discourage the idea of trying to *make it*. SAL MOSCA

I have people of all ages in my Sing Jazz classes, and every age is good. When you're young, if you're talented, you rely on your instincts. When you're older, you use your intelligence. Students often ask me if you need to have a trained voice. And the answer is, that the wonderful thing about jazz singing is that you do it with what you've got. So anybody can do it, who can do it. The notes you find you've got are part of the game. If you've only got five notes you learn to get the most out of them. So, I do ear training exercises and teach rudimentary harmony. Because a singer must always be able to *locate* notes from what your collaborators give you. We practise how to find your note whatever intro you may get – a lot of my classically trained students are completely thrown by a wild intro. Also, they often do not know how to establish a tempo to a collaborator.   JOY KANE

I have a rule in class. The piano player will not play until the student counts it off. And they don't believe me that this is crucial until they go out and sit in and mess up and come back and say, 'Oh, *wow*.'   JAY CLAYTON

But, amazingly enough, and this surprised me, you can teach rhythm, even to people who appear rather arhythmic. The game of taking as many risks as you can with the pulse and landing on your feet is unique to jazz. So we do exercises to build the rhythmic feel into the body, to imprint the sense of the eight-bar, four-bar phrase. I start to investigate improvisation – passing a musical thought round the room from person to person in eight-bar, four-bar phrases. I do exercises to make people more aware of the words, to add colour to sound. Because many singers, particularly those with an operatic training, think the words on the melodic line are just a vessel for the tonal quality of the voice. I also do exercises to awaken the actor, the expressive person, in a singer.

Now, what I can't teach. It's very hard to teach intonation, and this surprised me. I know what it is, so I thought I could teach it. But singers who are interested in self-display, display of their vocal equipment, are the singers who have intonation that doesn't match the intonation of their collaborators. It's a personality defect. They are just not listening.   JOY KANE

Clark Terry said that was what Duke was always telling the band, 'Listen, listen, listen.'   JOE LEE WILSON

To me, listening is the key to a musical education. I regard listening as more important than looking. In other words, it's more important that you *hear* the music you're going to sing than be able to read it. Because when you read it, you can only read what's there, so you can only *sing* what's there. But if you hear it, you can sing what's *felt*.   JON HENDRICKS

If I were coaching somebody I would tell them, if they were jazz directed, to listen to instrumentalists.   CHARLES COCHRAN

There's no standard way to sing. But there are standard principles we all follow. You have to work on the whole person, the physical, the spiritual, the emotional, the mental.   SAL MOSCA

Look, as long as it's musically all right, I really don't care how you breathe, where you sing *from*, the palate or the mask or whatever. Because from all parts of your body you can sing. It isn't necessarily right to breathe from the diaphragm, or open up the throat. I can't even agree that training helps to 'save' your voice. I know singers that have lessons, that keep taking lessons, that go to the most expensive throat specialists, but you give them a tour, forget it. They're on the floor. They still go under like the best of 'em. To me there is no right or wrong of it, see? None of the books and none of the teachers of all the things I ever learned in my whole life, which is a loooong time.   PEPI LEMER

I would try to teach you to be yourself. And not to do something that's been done a million times already.   SAL MOSCA

You've really got to reach in there and see what you've got.   JAY CLAYTON

In the end it comes down to the *will* to do it. Your voice won't fail you unless your head fails you. When it feels hard, it's probably the wrong song for you. Or you feel uncomfortable doing it. Then you don't have the confidence. So the throat will close up. And you'll start to wobble or whatever. Soon as the fear starts, forget it, the voice will go. You've got to get *past* the physical. And the mental. And let it be free.   PEPI LEMER

Many things hold you back from being Billie Holiday. For a start, your desire for music may not be as strong as it should be. It's almost as if you have to be *possessed* by it.   SAL MOSCA

I tell them, 'Learn how to live on little. Sometimes you have to reach in your pocket. Get part-time jobs. You've got to give things up for, maybe, twenty years.' Some people think that's very pessimistic. I think it's realistic.   JAY CLAYTON

I had a choice: to learn the technique of singing; and possibly to lose my feeling and my lustre and the libido, the id, the pulse, the strength that I had as a person who *felt* things, and losing the relationship of the song to *me*.   SYLVIA SYMS

You have to sit in. You have to gig and not get paid. You have to *get*

the gigs. You can't even sing for *nothing* at the beginning.   JAY
CLAYTON

And the important thing is to stop listening to the sound of your
voice and start listening to the sound of your heart.   SYLVIA SYMS

You must think about music all the time. It's got to be part of your
life.   SAL MOSCA

So, by the time it gets to be your turn, you will *be* whatever
individual it is that you are.   SYLVIA SYMS

7
With What?

*. . . they talk about the technology, and how you get to
hear them . . .*

I came along way back in BM – Before Microphones. MAXINE
SULLIVAN

These women just stood up and *sang*, that's what I saw them do. I
heard Ethel Waters one time – my mother took me to hear her. And
I went to the theatre and I caught Bessie Smith one time. And I
caught Ma Rainey one time. These women had voices, all right.
HELEN HUMES

The women learned the technique called 'throwing the velvet'. It's a
very particular technique to project the sound. ROSETTA REITZ

I sang in theatres the first time with Luis Russell's band, it must have
been about 1930. Of course, in those days, we didn't have any
amplification. So you had to sing with a natural singing voice, but
use it over the band. BILL DILLARD

They had megaphones – Jimmy Rushing used one. I could make
myself heard. I can. I do. It's to do with the way you use the voice.
A lot of times people tell me, 'Put that mike down and just
sing.' HELEN HUMES

Usually, when I walk away from the microphone and sing everybody's astounded, 'Oh my, there's a *real* voice.' At Carnegie Hall I
was with the big band doing Duke Ellington music and I didn't use
the microphone at all. CARRIE SMITH

I would be perfectly comfortable singing in a small room without a mike. But you'd have to have people really listening. SUSANNAH McCORKLE

You don't need to develop a real *voice* now, with the body mikes right under your chin and everything that they use. And the people at the console can make you heard anywhere. BILL DILLARD

Now singers depend totally on microphones. If there's no microphone, they can't perform. GRADY TATE

Many singers these days have virtually no voice at all: the technology does it for them. BILL DILLARD

The sound systems were very simple in the big band days. A piano mike. A mike in front of the band. In those days, you'd have a sixteen- or seventeen-piece band, with eight brass, five saxes. Now you have a three-piece band with seventeen or more stacked speakers. Making seventeen times the noise. CLEO LAINE

Christ, you stumble over mikes now all over the stage. *Drummers* have mikes. With my band in the forties, we had one mike out front, that's all. That was for me singing. And Sarah would come out, the band would come out and take their solos at the mike. BILLY ECKSTINE

We've had microphones since – when? – the middle thirties? And you *still* take a chance every time you get up there. In most clubs you get the worst p.a. systems. I guess that's why a lot of established singers take their own p.a. CARRIE SMITH

Wherever, whoever you may be, the sound system isn't always just so. It happens at every level. I went to hear Lena Horne the other day and the mike went out. It happens all the time. BOBBY SHORT

I like to do a long sound check. People get very angry with me because I spend time doing it. And I say, 'To hell with you', because I feel it is so important. It's crucial to me to be able to hear myself properly on the monitors and get the right level of sound. Too much amplification intimidates the audience, too little and they're going to lose interest. CLEO LAINE

Those sound checks – oh God, they look like you're going to the electric chair out there, all those wires all over the stage. And it doesn't necessarily sound no different – just louder. BILLY ECKSTINE

Every place is different. Some halls are built for acoustic music: you shouldn't have too much amplification, there's so much brightness. You need just enough to get the sound of the group across, using the acoustic of the hall. Then you get a bathroomy sound when you rehearse in a room with a lot of glass or wood or concrete, and you need to know if the sound is different when it's full of people. And if the room is full of curtains and carpeting, the sound is dead: so it's going to be even deader with people there, so you need a bit of brightener, echo or whatever, in the sound system.   CLEO LAINE

Without a microphone, Billie Holiday would never have had a career.   BILL DILLARD

I don't feel it's a crutch – it's an integral part of one's sound.   SUSANNAH McCORKLE

Now that I've accepted it, I love it. It's my instrument.   JAY CLAYTON

Mike technique I've learned just from experience. It's like working to a camera if you're a film actor.   SHEILA JORDAN

You use the microphone to find your sound.   JAY CLAYTON

There are lots of things you can do with a microphone that you couldn't possibly do with the naked voice.   NORMA WINSTONE

That whisper that almost became my trademark – it's a sound that wouldn't exist without the microphone. I was able to use the microphone closely: it was something I discovered. I mean, it came along, and other sounds, many other sounds, as an expressive device. The microphone becomes an extension of your instrument, whether it's Miles' trumpet, or my voice.   HELEN MERRILL

I know by now what a microphone will or will not do for me. I know with the right microphone and the amplification and the monitor I can get a certain sound that pleases my ear. Most people need a microphone to make them sound warm and beautiful. I'm very, very bassy – I need something to give me a bit of edge. Sometimes I can sound like I've got cotton-wool balls in my mouth on certain parts of my range.   CLEO LAINE

Now they have these horrible microphones, that everyone swears by, that you have to *kiss* while you're singing. If you're not eating everyone else's germs, you're not heard. If you move your head to the left or right or back, you're off-mike.   HELEN MERRILL

Another thing, the technicians often aren't used to a singer who uses such a wide range of voice as I do – and the mike has to cope with all of that.   CLEO LAINE

I have to rely on a microphone because I don't have a big sound. So if it's a bad one, a lot of the subtleties just don't come out, which can be a drag.   SHEILA JORDAN

If you have to project for loudness, it changes your concept. It's the difference between saying a very subtle, gentle thing and using a powerful projection. It kind of contradicts what you're saying.   JAY CLAYTON

I like to be able to *whisper* and still be able to hear everything.   NORMA WINSTONE

The microphone is not crucial to the things I do at all. I'd rather form the sound in myself. I've been working on it all for quite a while.   BOBBY McFERRIN

When I do solo gigs, I like to work both on- and off- mike. I like to explore the different sounds, both acoustic and miked. And I like to move, too.   MAGGIE NICOLS

I've gotten pretty frisky in my latter years – I find myself damn near kneeling on the floor sometimes. I started using a hand mike – and I should have done it long ago, because I've always moved a lot.   SHEILA JORDAN

I used to use two hand mikes a lot on live gigs. One was to do sound effects, the other to sing straight. Sometimes I used both at the same time, with distortion on one of them – you get a spill of the voice which you can play with. Sometimes the sound is an echo or a reverb, sometimes a sound to change the mood of the music, that will drive the music somewhere else, like a sign, you know. Or it's to let the band know my feelings at the time. I used to think it was all purely improvised, but I calculated it too, you know.   FLORA PURIM

That's why I like the omni-directional mike. Because you can control your sound by the movement of your head, moving closer or away. So it's more creative.   HELEN MERRILL

I'd like to work without a microphone, because it is very limiting. My goal is solo voice concerts. And I'd just want a mike from the ceiling – like when an operatic singer does a recital – the *environ-*

134

ment is miked. Then I wouldn't be confined to one spot. BOBBY McFERRIN

All musicians listen to one another, as you know. And Miles Davis told me he was fascinated by my low notes and the way I'd make them close to the microphone. And Miles told me that he copied that from me – that close mike sound. He copied my sound. And then he developed it to where it became history, as you know. HELEN MERRILL

At this point I'm not fascinated by the technical procedures. I would rather spend my time just improvising. BOBBY McFERRIN

★

Records are like calling cards. Once you've got a record out, you can send it round, so people who have not yet come to hear you know you exist. JEANNE LEE

Three minutes. It's such a small part of a person's life. And yet a three-minute side of a record could change someone's life and career. Or change someone's life on the other side of the world when they heard it. See, I knew that. I used to say, 'Let's make one more take, it's only three minutes.' I was famous for that. That was my big line. MILT GABLER

My story is on records; the sound of my voice at different times in my life. ABBEY LINCOLN

In a way, the recorded sound is the *real* sound for most people. Most people who buy a record may never hear the person live. CHARLES COCHRAN

You can never pick the day you want to make the record. MOSE ALLISON

I know you can be so relaxed, and you go into the studio and you're so happy to be there at that piano. And the instant the light goes on, you get *petrified*. And your fingers don't want to move. You just get that feeling, '*Move*, fingers.' And your voice chokes up. You want it to be *perfect*, because that's how you're judged, and sometimes that scares you to death. ROSE MURPHY

Recording is a structure, a tight structure. The way the structure is set up it's very confining. There's a man sitting in a booth, like judge and jury. And you've got to *please*. Someone, other than you, says, 'That was a good take' or 'Let's do it again.' You're not in charge.

Someone else is putting a value on it. And there's a microphone staring you in the face. Even when you hear it back, *it's not like you.* It's not like you hear yourself.   BARNEY KESSEL

If you can negotiate a producer-artist contract, you feel so much better. When, even if it's a piece of crap, it's the piece of crap *you* want.   LEON THOMAS

If you listen to a tape you always notice the things that you don't like about it more than the things that are good about it.   BETTY SMITH

You really think you're singing your *buns* off until you hear it back.   GEORGE SHEARING

A lot of times you're inhibited in a studio, because you know that everything you do is going to be thrown back at you. On a live performance, once you've done it, it's gone.   GRADY TATE

It's very different from live singing. You must not give it as much. A good recording mike will pick up every nuance, so you must under-play.   CHARLES COCHRAN

Normally, I can't stand to hear a *live* recorded performance of mine. Because it's usually slightly over the top. Because the performance comes into it more. And then you think, 'Oh God, how could I have done that.'   ELAINE DELMAR

A gig is a gig. A recording is a finished product. There'll be another gig. There won't be another recording session, and it's got to be better than good.   JOHNNY M

It's *better* than a gig. I remember the very first time I recorded. Everyone was so worried about me – would I freeze up, etcetera? And I was really happy. Because no one was talking. It was the first time I'd ever sung publicly, when no one, *no one*, was talking.   SUSANNAH McCORKLE

I come over better in person than on records. I can't explain it, because there are so many people that are captured on records: their whole soul is on the record. And I can't understand why they can't capture me. It's not how I think I am.   CARRIE SMITH

If I have a style, it's from listening to my own recordings and discarding the things that I didn't like and keeping the things that I did like.   ROSEMARY CLOONEY

I think I have perfected some of the intonation and some of the vocal and musical approach through listening to myself on tape and being totally *devastated* by some of the things that I heard.   GEORGE SHEARING

If you hit the wrong phrasing it's just painful to hear it back. So you become more disciplined and more accurate.   JULIE AMIET

When I was with Basie I'd record everything, rehearsals, shows. And after the gig I'd lie in bed and play it back and think, oh, don't ever do *that* again.   JOE WILLIAMS

When ECM recorded me, it was the first time I really began to like the sound of my voice, and to be able to listen to it without being embarrassed. So I began to make my voice *sound* like that – do you know what I mean?   NORMA WINSTONE

You can find you get tonal qualities you didn't even know you had just by listening to the play-back, and using different breathing techniques, different ways of using the microphone.   JULIE AMIET

And it's an amazing sound you can get. I love it. I love the sensitivity.   CAROL KIDD

One thing that I found out, and it surprised me, was that you can hear a smile on a record. A warmth comes through, when you smile.   ROSEMARY CLOONEY

But if you dwell on your recorded sound too much you're going to get self-conscious, I think. You have to let go of that. And get into the song.   CHARLES COCHRAN

I know the record business has changed. I haven't made a record in a studio for years. But my last record was done at the Nice Festival last year, right out in the open. No studio at all. We just played. And they recorded it. And, you know, we did it just the way my very first record was made in the forties.   ROSE MURPHY

It's come full circle, hasn't it? You now have companies advertising 'Direct to Disc' recording, as if it was new. And it's just the same way we made records back in the thirties.   MILT GABLER

A recording is an *artefact*. To think of it as anything else is a romantic fantasy.   JERRY WEXLER

Here's how I did it. I'd listen to the singers many, many times in the places they worked. I'd find the songs I wanted to do, or I'd hear a singer do something I wanted to record. I'd find the musicians to back the singer, and I'd choose musicians the singer liked, so the singer would be inspired. Then, they'd all be in the one room all at the same instant. And the singer would listen to everything the musicians were doing as they ran the arrangement. And they'd be listening to what the singer did. The men would group themselves the proper distance from the mike, for a balance, and you would have a mike for the rhythm section – the bass players weren't using amplifiers in those days. The singer's mike was a little off to the side, so everyone could see, but the rhythm section wouldn't get into the vocal mike too much, but the singer could hear them. This was before recording with earphones on. And you were making a *record* of what they would play in a live situation. And it was all finished in forty-five minutes or so. And, of course, there was an edge, a performance edge. That's why these people were so great. You wouldn't have them there if they weren't. And that's why those records are so great. Classics.   MILT GABLER

I hadn't heard myself at all until that first record of mine was in the shops. I heard it and I said, 'Ooh, that's not *me*.'   ROSE MURPHY

You couldn't hear play-backs in the old days. If you played back an acetate or a wax disc, you would destroy it – the needle would cut the groove up. So when you told Bing or Billie Holiday or Coleman Hawkins, 'That's it', they had to trust you. They believed you, if you knew what you were doing. And they never heard it until the record came out. And you found out whether you were right or wrong.   MILT GABLER

These days you hear these producers say, '*I* made this record.'   BILLY ECKSTINE

The engineers, they think of themselves as the artist. The music is just components they put together. The voice is just another instrument they can manipulate.   GRADY TATE

If you can find someone to invest money in you and you have a fair voice, they will spend money to have arrangements made, to have a coach work on whatever recording you're going to make; they will get the best sound studio with twenty tracks, to control the slightest sound from each instrument. They can play about with it afterwards, rerecord, cut out the bad bits – they can make your voice sound gorgeous.   BILL DILLARD

I know why these recording singers do a phrase at a time, punch in,

138

punch out. They want to get a good composite thing. But when you hear the person in person, they don't sound like the record.   BILLY ECKSTINE

It is the absolute opposite of what a performance *is*.   GRADY TATE

I'm not too fascinated with the recording process yet. I really believe in the art of improvisation. More than anything. The music of the moment happens one time. And that's it. Here's the problem I have with recording. As much as I enjoyed doing my first album, a lot of it was pieced together. Not like an actual perform-ance.   BOBBY McFERRIN

You do it all through the cans, the earphones, these days. And you can't get the music through the earphones so you can't hear just what's going to be on the record. So you've got to pretend so much, pretend that you're hearing the end product, what you want to hear.   MARK MURPHY

I find I can't improvise very well after the band's gone, when I'm just singing to a backing track blasting through the earphones. I need musicians. I can't bear it when they're not there.   JULIE AMIET

If you work to a rhythm track, the singer is trapped by whatever the producer decided when the track was made. Even the musicians are. It makes a difference to the feeling.   MILT GABLER

Everything is done dry. Your voice has no natural overtones. Music has to have natural overtones. That's how you hear me now, because there are sounds travelling in the room. They stop all that. And then they say 'We'll get it in the mix.' But you can't mix what isn't there on the tape. They can't put it on later. They've lost the natural tones that float around. You can learn to function as that kind of singer, but it doesn't do my kind of singer any good. Because essentially I'm doing a live performance.   HELEN MERRILL

Now, on that recording we did last night with Bob Moses, I was listening like a craftsman, not a listener, and concentrating on making the appropriate tonal rhythms. Bob made about six tracks. I know there are two tracks I'm on, plus the track with the other singers, plus another track with bass clarinet, plus the one with the long drums and the bass, plus a percussion track, each made one on top of the other, so everyone is listening to everyone else's work and adding their own thing on top. And at one point there are three microphones, each with two singers per mike, plus me with the solo. They did the riff, and I had to sing a melody line in my lower register that would connect up. Then, for my second over-dub, I had to join the riff, but make it all from aspirated sounds, rhythms and tones. And when we all came back and listened to the play-back, it was *something else* – you know how they say something is more than the sum of its parts. Nothing had to be retaken, it was unbelievable. All the singers were so full of respect for the space, no one, in spite of all the talent that was there, oversang. What Moses had done in construction was the unifying factor. It was the most magical recording date I've been on.   JEANNE LEE

I would say high technology is not for our kind of music – *my* kind of music. People like me should always do two-track recording. In fact, I produced a singer, Ann Burton, in Holland. And we did it two-track. We went straight ahead, and I got the balance in the room. I said, 'Yes, put a little more high on the bass; put a little tiny echo on the piano, because it loses in the pressing.' And what we heard, was what you got on the record. And it got an award in Holland.   HELEN MERRILL

I did a record with Carmen McRae last year. Just piano and voice. We never rehearsed. I hit a chord, and she was *there*. The whole album was completed, start to finish, in three hours and forty-five minutes. Most of it is first takes. You tell *that* to one of the present-day, would-be stars.   GEORGE SHEARING

It's hard to build a large following without making record-ings.   ABBEY LINCOLN

You need a hit record so people will come to see you work.   MILT GABLER

We recorded 'Let Me off Uptown' in 1941. Gene Krupa used to tell people it was the biggest hit he ever had . . . With that hit record, it seemed almost everyone's attitude towards me suddenly changed . . . Roy's name and mine were both used, so suddenly everybody was saying, 'Hi, Anita.' My privacy was gone. I'd go into some dumb bar, as was my habit, to have a drink, and the first thing I knew somebody'd spot me and want me to sign a matchbook or a soggy napkin. I didn't mind. I loved it, gloried in it, basked in it. I'd achieved my goal.   ANITA O'DAY

There's no better publicity than a hit record.   MILT GABLER

140

Of course, I got stuck with 'Loch Lomond'. It was Number One for a long time. I'm *still* stuck with it. As far as I was concerned it was just luck. The voice was different, and it was a novelty, the folk song thing. It was all Claude Thornhill's idea. I became a star. More than a star, I was a *comet.* And I got just twenty-five dollars for it. Just like everyone else.   MAXINE SULLIVAN

Dick Haymes had just left Harry James and he did a song for us called 'You'll Never Know', for seventy-five dollars. And it sold a million. He got three hundred dollars for an afternoon's work, and he thought that was pretty good. But, because of that hit, he got a Hollywood contract for twenty-five thousand dollars a year.   MILT GABLER

I did a demo record for a fellow in Philadelphia and he sent it to Peggy Lee. She heard it with an A & R man from Capitol Records. And she turned to him and said, 'Forget the song, and get the singer.' And he did. And I got a contract.   MARIAN MONTGOMERY

I made several albums. Because they're old and out of print, people are paying a lot of money for them, as they do with a lot of obscure artists, which is what I like to call myself.   BOBBY COLE

I would say my records are not representative at all. I find the record business has now deteriorated to a form of prostitution.   JON HENDRICKS

I got my album *Edge of Time* because I'd won the *Melody Maker* poll, and they thought *someone* must like her. I could have told them it wouldn't be commercial. And no one could find it in the shops, either.   NORMA WINSTONE

You won't find my records in most record shops. I know it's a drag carrying them round with you. But the people I sing for are quite delighted to get a record at the same time they hear me. So I say, 'Take me home with you tonight. On record.'   BERYL BRYDEN

I've been ripped off so long, recording is unimportant to me right now. I do records in every country. I never get the royalties. I never got them in my life. But, you need records.   JIMMY WITHERSPOON

There are about thirty companies issuing the old stuff of mine, and I only get royalties from one. I've sent nice letters. I've sent legal letters. I've called them on the phone. You walk into a store, say, in Europe, see your record bright as day. No royalties, nothing.

Song royalties, yes, because you're an ASCAP member. Artist's? Nothing. Zero. Blank.   SLIM GAILLARD

Any artist got a flat fee in those days. When their records are reissued, they get nothing. They're not entitled.   MILT GABLER

There's one company in Tokyo releasing all the sides I ever made in my entire life, sent me a letter, 'We are so happy to have you as a member of our group.' All these companies, expanding, building new office buildings. *You* tell me what to do.   SLIM GAILLARD

As much as the record company is doing for me as far as publicity is concerned, and getting me a chance to work in different countries and travel, it also has a tendency to work against me. And I'm kind of frightened about that. Because the record company wants me to do things that they can sell. And then they want me to repeat what has been selling. And, as much as I want to be successful and support my family like any normal human being does, I don't see it as being successful if I have to sacrifice my own self.   BOBBY McFERRIN

Well, if it hadn't been for the record company, you wouldn't know me. And I wouldn't be sitting here. Chances are, if I'd been, say a piano player, I'd have been passed over, just as oodles of them are passed over. It's because of *this* instrument, the popularity of the voice and the lyric. It's because of the *voice* they took that chance on me.   AL JARREAU

142

8
Why Not?

. . . they talk about what goes wrong . . .

I'm fifty years old and I have no more home, no more kids, no more family. I was married for twenty-three years. And nobody's around any more. It sounds melodramatic, but that's exactly the size of it. And I lost my wife and my family and my kids, because they *accommodated* me, bless 'em, all those years. And finally they just couldn't accommodate me any more.   BOBBY COLE

Sometimes you can miss out on a lot of the other things in life because you're so caught up in it, the music.   JULIE AMIET

I can't think about anything else, never could. The people I've been with have been very jealous of the music. And the music is part of me. If you find somebody who knows what you're into and tries to pull you away from it, you'll let that person go.   SHEILA JORDAN

Well, what happened to me was I was married. And the fellow that I married, he knew that I wanted a career. Everything was fine when we were courting, he was behind me one hundred per cent. But, when I started really moving, then it became a problem. And I had to choose. Did I want to have a home and a family, or did I want a career? And I wanted a career.   CARRIE SMITH

It's an old story in show business and it happens all the time, doesn't it? The woman's career takes off and her management says, 'Do this. Do that. You don't need him.' But if he knows who he is and he is not threatened by what you want to become and he doesn't feel that he has to impose his will on you – if it's an equal partnership

143

thing – then it can be wonderful. Who is in your corner, supposedly, more than your spouse? BARBARA CARROLL

I suppose a lot of men are attracted to you because of what you do. You're special, you know. And they would like to be with somebody special. But can they handle that? Once they get into that special world, can they deal with it? A lot of us singers have a particular attitude about things, and men can't handle it. They can't handle the aggressiveness. I know they can't handle *my* aggressiveness. Because I know I'm aggressive. BETTY CARTER

The thing that drives people apart is success. Because when you become successful, you become very independent. JACKIE CAIN

People can force you apart, even if you're compatible – managers, business, travelling. ROY KRAL

I'm not sure whether it's possible to have a really normal family life and a career as a singer. I'm not sure about that. MAXINE SULLIVAN

I went through years and years of apologizing for being what I am and doing what I do. I wasn't the regular father. I didn't get out and toss the old ball around with the boy. Because I have to watch my hands. And I have to learn another song. BOBBY COLE

When I came to London, I got married, got pregnant and went on tour for about five months when the child was very young. And it was too much for me and I got ill and I got the nesting urge and relinquished all my contacts in the United States, and it was probably the biggest single mistake I ever made in my life. MARIAN MONTGOMERY

To pursue a singing career you really have to travel. It was all right when I could take everybody with me. I lived all over the world with my children when they were very small. But then, in the midst of it, when they started school, I found myself being torn, because I was away for a long time. I wasn't giving my full attention to my work *or* the children. So I was treading water. And not really getting anywhere. And not feeling very good about it either. ROSEMARY CLOONEY

I don't do so many club dates since I had my two smaller children. Because you cannot sing in a club all night and then come home and take good care of two small kids. I tend to do more concerts and workshops these days. JEANNE LEE

144

I've been in the business about thirty-three years, and I've always had a family life. I was married for ten of those years, and in my early period, my husband was around to help out. My family was not too keen on what I was doing, but my friends managed to find people to help me take care of my babies when they were small. And I had boys. I don't know how it would have worked out with girls.   BETTY CARTER

I have three kids. I get up at three o'clock in the morning. They're asleep. It's quiet. I finally have my own space. I don't have to clean. I don't have to cook. I don't have to do the laundry. And I just sit and enjoy the silence. And sometimes it's the most precious time of the day for me. As much as I enjoy my family.   JEANNE LEE

I think I've got quite good at switching on and off into various rôles through having the children and wanting to do the right things by them, as I see it, but at the same time not wanting to give up *anything*. I try to cut myself in half. Ralph Towner said, when we did a tour with him, 'I see you suddenly *change*. There you are, with the children, a Mum, at rehearsal, and then you suddenly switch to another gear.' And I find I can completely *forget* them. I just don't think about them. I *can't*.   NORMA WINSTONE

You have to go out there and suddenly be *yourself.*   JAY CLAYTON

People who I respect totally have said you can have a family *or* you can have a career. And they have chosen to have a career. But for me I am totally immersed in what's around me. Yes, I need my moment of being alone, to dig in and synthesize. But my work is part of my life. And my family is part of my life. And my work feeds my life. And my life feeds my work. And it's up to me to organize it so one action serves many directions.   JEANNE LEE

We've had rough moments a couple of times, you know. We almost split up.   JACKIE CAIN

We've also been out of the business several times – about a year and a half with each child. And then, being in Las Vegas – I count that as being out of the business – because we both wanted to be at home and not travel. Then we did commercials for about five years too.   ROY KRAL

When the children were school age, it would have been easier if one of us was working and the other was home. Working *together* made it very difficult sometimes.   JACKIE CAIN

Now we're totally free once more. Our time is our own. And I guess we have a good segment of the American Dream.   ROY KRAL

Sometimes your family supports you monetarily, and sometimes you support your family. But it's a support system in other ways. It's the people that care about you, whether you've given a good performance or not.   JEANNE LEE

Maybe to do it right, you have to give up your personal life; ruthless helps. I'm not willing to do that. I like both. That's been my biggest problem. I care much more about the people close to me than whether people out there love me – those fly-by-night faces, who like you when you're popular, and then don't like you when you're not popular.   HELEN MERRILL

Being a mother is a lot of work. Our two kids are fourteen months apart. And to tell you the truth, I don't know *how* Frank and I managed. Once they're five and six, it starts to get heavy financially, you need a bigger place to live, all that. And our income still goes up and down, after twenty years of actual performing. I'm still doing those fifty-dollar gigs.   JAY CLAYTON

People say to me, 'Well, you haven't *suffered*.' How do they know? I don't think you can assess people on their tragic life, or whatever. You can only assess them on what they've done with the gift they've got.   CLEO LAINE

If there was someone who would be bad for me, I would find that man. *Why?* I think a lot of creative women are like this. And I think the only thing that saves us is the art.   SHEILA JORDAN

I was a young woman who was looking for a husband. I was singing to make a living. And, when I first started singing, I would look up and down the bar, to see if he was there. And he never was. But sometimes I would think he was there. I wasn't interested in a career, I didn't know anything about a career. I was interested in finding a man to be with.   ABBEY LINCOLN

I think I'm more in charge of my life now than I ever have been. When I was younger I had a tendency to listen exclusively to the person who was in charge, without trusting my own judgement enough. And I think that was a mistake at various times in my life. But that was part of the female conditioning of the fifties. That was what we were supposed to *do*.   ROSEMARY CLOONEY

★

146

Pitfalls? Drugs and alcohol – that's the only pitfalls in this business worth talking about.   BOBBY COLE

We all find ways to try to destroy ourselves. Drugs – it was the rage. It's still the rage. It's the rage when you're not happy, not confident, when you can't deal with life. It's a death wish. I'm speaking from what I *know*, not something I've read.   SHEILA JORDAN

I get drugs offered to me every fifteen minutes. Why? People like drugs. A lot of them are pushers and they want to get me hooked. Others do it because misery loves company.   BOBBY COLE

Looking back, I also realize that I was always alone, fending for myself, doing the best I could without the family support a seven-teen-year-old ordinarily gets. Smoking pot, drinking, playing it cool were my ways of hiding the pain and deprivation I wouldn't let myself realize . . . So I drank, got high, learned to cover up my feelings of pain beneath a hip, swinging-chick personality I'd care-fully developed.   ANITA O'DAY

One of the reasons I drank is that I didn't think I would have any confidence if I put down that drink.   SHEILA JORDAN

And there's a need sometimes to take a couple of drinks to relax before a show. If you can leave it at that . . .   HELEN MERRILL

I was always the one that kept sober, so I could drive them home, when *they* got drunk.   HELEN HUMES

When you're not working, that's when the temptations can arise. When you're not making music.   HELEN MERRILL

The show's over and nothing's happening. You try to make it continue. The curtain goes down, you go home to a hotel room. There's nothing there. I used to drink to forget. And I did.   ANITA O'DAY

And the more drugs you do, the more paranoid you get. Someone says, 'Hello', and you want to start a fight.   BOBBY COLE

Yes, it's very likely that to have a lasting career as a singer you must give up most of the things you like. Singing is physical, *per se*. You take care of yourself, or you can't do it.   BOBBY SHORT

You have to keep in shape, because you never know when that phone's going to ring.   LEON THOMAS

People wonder why singers can be neurotic, and why they are

difficult when they, quote, make it. Or why they take to the things it's so easy to take to.   ANNIE ROSS

It's a daily battle to imitate straight life. So I make this daily effort to keep myself your common, ordinary B flat human being.   HELEN MERRILL

★

The business of opening your mouth and singing is a natural act. It's instinctive. But the business of singing as a career, isn't instinctive.   CLEO LAINE

Singing is the easy part. Trying to make a living out of it, that's the hard part. The audience doesn't know what you have to go through just to *get* the gig.   CHRIS CONNOR

Everybody wants you to sing for free.   JOE LEE WILSON

The hardest part is surviving in this business. And being able to pay your bills.   SYLVIA SYMS

The majority doesn't go to see jazz singers.   MIKE McKENZIE

You do music the way you do music, your own way. And it's not acceptable. And there's no place to do it. No place to sing. No place to express yourself. And you have this extreme need to give this gift, 'Take this, take it from me, I want to give you this, I want you to feel what I'm feeling, I want to *sing.*' And you can't do it. You can become very negative about everything.   SHEILA JORDAN

Everyone lives hand-to-mouth, of course. Every time you go looking for work, it's as if you've never achieved anything. People who have been around for years.   PEPI LEMER

You either have to play little bitty clubs for five hundred dollars, or at least be a three-thousand-dollar-a-week act. That means you can work all the time if you're an unknown or a Peggy Lee.   ANITA O'DAY

My agent says if you play the little places you won't get the big places.   GEORGIE FAME

There is no *demand* for jazz singers. You have to create your own market place. You have to find places, persuade them that it would be a good thing to have you there, then you have to find an audience and then you have to touch an audience. There's a whole bunch of things that have to happen together.   JOHNNY M

148

These plantation owners – it's not my term – they know the hard time jazz musicians have and they take advantage of it. 'You want the job? You work for the money I'm offering you.' Which is sometimes the money they were offering twenty-five years ago.   MARILYN MOORE

. . . all of the humiliations of being – *cheated*, you know. When I did deps in East End pubs, I'd get my pay envelope and it was always short. I'd always have to open it up on the spot and say, 'Look, you said such and such, and this is only –' Or you show for a gig and they'd say, 'Oh, we're not having music any more.' Once you get a name and start working in a little better places, it doesn't happen quite so much. But there are horror stories all up and down the line.   SUSANNAH McCORKLE

Nothing's going to come to you. You got to go out and get it.   JOE LEE WILSON

You've got to hustle. There were times I spent more time on the phone, lining up jobs, than playing the music.   ROY KRAL

Years ago, when I first started playing, I'd be getting dressed, and the make-up and the bright lights, the whole thing, this was exciting too. But since then, I've realized this is hard work. I'm a kind of low-key person, so I didn't really push for it. It's hard to sell yourself as a product. I had a good husband, you know so I never really had to work. I could be picky. But that's not the way to build a career-type name, you know.   SHIRLEY HORN

You know, I've had so many people tell me, 'Helen, you're not bitchy enough.' I say, 'Well, what do you mean?' 'I mean, you're so easygoing, you're supposed to raise hell and tell them this and that and the other.' And I say, 'If that's what you have to do, well, just forget about *me*.'   HELEN HUMES

Some people have a hard time getting started. But the middle part, when you come off a huge success, is hard. When people say, 'What are you going to do *next*?' It was the hardest part for me.   ROSEMARY CLOONEY

I had not made up my mind to be a singer. Six months after I won the Amateur Hour at the Apollo, I was in California, nine months later on tour in Europe, with a record, and I thought, oh, I'm a singer. I had a career. And I left it after the European tour because I wanted to reassess, you know. Things were beyond my control. I was a product. I was being moved around. And I was told that my feelings about my personal development were not important. JEANNE LEE

After doing all those awful gigs, I decided that if that's all there *was* I didn't want to know. I thought, no, I'd sooner not sing at all. So for a couple of years I stopped singing in public at all. And I thought, I'd just work out the programme I'd like to do if I was ever allowed to do it. I'd realized by this time that what I was obviously trying to do was jazz, and none of those people were interested in it. So I gave up. NORMA WINSTONE

I get a lot of support from musicians; they're like my brothers and dear friends, and they've helped me when I've been down. Roger Sellers used to say, 'If you haven't got any gigs, just prepare yourself for the ones you're going to have.' It's easy to do nothing and say you're going to do everything and drink a lot and smoke a lot. JULIE AMIET

That's when you need faith in your life. It's a matter of maintaining your spirit. ABBEY LINCOLN

I would find a tune in the fake book and I would play it – dumb chords – and I would transpose it into my key and write it out. All those *motions* for me meant I was doing something. JAY CLAYTON

There have been times in my life when I have hoped that life would *not* go on. I would be a fool if I said I've just sat around and laughed all the time. I've had some crying times. And my career has taken some very, very wild forks in the road, sometimes to oblivion. But if you hang in there long enough, you come out smelling like a rose, maybe. SYLVIA SYMS

It's easier for girls. There's more men in the business at the hiring end, promoters, club-owners, whatever. And they look at a girl for more than her singing, that's for sure. A guy says, 'If I'm going to give you a job, what am *I* going to get out of it?' I'm not saying that the ladies *have* to distribute their favours, but I'm saying that's a part of getting ahead. JOE LEE WILSON

To make it as an artist, you've got to be very self-serving. MARILYN MOORE

★

Theoretically, a singer married to her manager should be the most beautiful thing. So how come it's not, most of the time? BARBARA CARROLL

150

This is one of the things where Bessie made her mistake. She was doing fine, and then along comes Charlie Gee. She marries him, and he wants to be her manager all of a sudden, and he doesn't know one thing about managing *anything*.   CARRIE SMITH

That's been the big problem for many singers. Sometimes they seem to have confidence in the wrong people.   JIMMY ROWLES

If anyone has stars in the eyes, they should have a manager. It's more difficult to talk for yourself. Unless you just want to sit back and take a few engagements here and there, that you get called back for.   PETER DEAN

Managers are a bunch of thieves too.   JIMMY WITHERSPOON

It's better for me to be doing it myself. So I sit here and type letters and my phone bill goes up and up and up. Someone who will work for you is worth his weight in gold. But they often don't have the time to really devote to you.   BERYL BRYDEN

I don't have a manager and I don't want one at this stage. I think I do a better job, I'm more on top of things. It would be nice to be protected, you know, but I haven't found anyone yet.   SUSANNAH McCORKLE

Some people need that, need someone who will give them instructions, guidance, act as a buffer against the rest of the outside world. It's very hard to hustle your own gigs, sell yourself.   BARBARA CARROLL

I feel funny naming a price for myself at a club. I try to divorce myself from *myself*. I try to think, now, I'm an agent, then, I'm the artist.   SUSANNAH McCORKLE

I have a modest income, but I also have modest and realistic goals. I've had my share of scuffling. I've had success. I handle all my business, and now I do pretty much what I want to do.   HELEN MERRILL

Musicians should all take business administration courses. Basically, artists *feel* everything. If it don't feel right, they don't do it. But business has nothing to do with feelings.   JOE LEE WILSON

When trad jazz became commercial in the early sixties, a friend, who was a City broker, went round and got me work in smart nightclubs as a jolly old jazz singer, because it was all in the Hit

Parade here at the time. He thought I had great potential as an *international star*.   BERYL BRYDEN

A manager will take any job for you as long as he gets the commission. He'll wear you out, send you anywhere, without thinking about your expenses when you're travelling. You've got to pay for food, hotel, transport, you know.   JIMMY WITHERSPOON

He was reluctant to contact the jazz festivals and places I wanted to work. And he would get me things like working men's clubs up North, which paid good money, but had combos, not jazz bands, so you had to work from written-out parts, and you got the same backing all the time. He got me into big hotels as a cabaret artist. But, you know, there's no kick at all for a jazz singer just to be wearing a beautiful gown and walking round the audience singing 'A Good Man is Hard to Find' at some bald head in the front row.   BERYL BRYDEN

First thing a manager tries to do is change you. They even get into your private life if they can, tell you what to do, not to do.   JIMMY WITHERSPOON

Somebody you meet wants to be a part of your career and work as your manager. They find you wonderful. But it's like when you get married sometimes. After you start to be their client they start trying to reshape things.   ABBEY LINCOLN

In the end what it always boils down to is – does the manager work for the artist, or does the artist work for the manager?   BERYL BRYDEN

If you have to have a manager, just make sure to choose someone with *money*.   JOE LEE WILSON

You might have a manager who knows more about what's going on out there than you do. And he might move you to another type of singing. And you might become a star.   JULIA STEELE

The way the industry is built up, in terms of mystiques and stars and all, is really apart from the *fact* of being a musician.   JEANNE LEE

But record companies will have you believe that either you're a *superstar* or forget it, you won't work. It's scary. I'm frightened, I don't mind saying that.   BOBBY McFERRIN

So you don't try to compete in a market place that is based on having only *one* up there at a time. You find out where you fit in the community, in the schools, colleges, in the museums, in the churches, the music clubs. And you work with a non-profit arts organization or an arts management group.   JEANNE LEE

Some of us are cult singers. And being a cult singer is a very strange space to be in. But I think every jazz singer has to look for that, ultimately.   MARK MURPHY

I've got this sort of minor cult thing abroad. It's amazing really, but of course it's taken years and years to build up and it could disappear any moment. I've also had periods on social security, no work at all.   MAGGIE NICOLS

Sometimes people are on you. Sometimes they're off you. Sometimes you get the work. Sometimes sombody else is doing it.   SALENA JONES

As I've started getting some really good breaks, I find there are other pressures. Professional jealousies, tension, strain. I think it's kind of silly, because no one is going to get rich and famous from this kind of music.   SUSANNAH McCORKLE

The nature of this business is such that, if you're not a neurotic you're some sort of superhuman. Because it's a very insecure business, and, in many instances, unrewarded. Unless you're a top performer. And there are very few top performers. And these people are not usually jazz singers. But if you are, you can carry your sound people, lighting people and you can hire someone to do all your shouting for you.   GRADY TATE

If you go into this music thinking you're going to raise roof-tops and make all kinds of bread, it's ridiculous. Anyone who goes into it for those reasons might as well stay out.   SHEILA JORDAN

Singing has to be more important to you than any kind of hope or any kind of money or any kind of wisdom. Or any kinds of drugs or booze. That's how you keep it together.   SYLVIA SYMS

And you have to *outlive* the entrepreneurs and the industry. So it's a matter of endurance, and continually honing your craft, and finding the strength and courage and understanding to go to the same well for your sustenance, and not run to some poisoned little creek, because you're afraid.   ABBEY LINCOLN

I sing for my supper. Quite literally.   BOBBY COLE

If you are able to withstand the extreme temperature changes that

come in your life, the emotional upheavals, and the disappoint-
ments and the surprises, and even the rewards; if you can maintain
an even road, eventually you can have the ear of the world. Even
sometimes after you've passed away.   ABBEY LINCOLN

9
Lady

. . . they talk about a great jazz voice . . .

I came into this club in Harlem, early 1933, and there was a chubby beautiful young girl singing, and she was doing the table-hopping routine. She would sing a chorus at one table and then another. And I listened, and to my astonishment, she sang a completely different chorus to the same tune at each table. It was the first really improvising singer that I had heard.   JOHN HAMMOND

I didn't know her before the Hot-cha Club in Harlem. It's a burned-out building now. And every time I pass it, I can't help but think of Billie Holiday.   BILL DILLARD

. . . a young healthy kid only about seventeen or so at the time I first met her, but already beginning to develop that distinctive style of hers which has been copied and imitated by so many singers of popular music, that the average listener of today cannot realize how original she actually is. For she has had so many imitators that, even if you are hearing her for the first time, it is as if you were listening to someone you've been hearing for a long, long time.   ARTIE SHAW

We tend to forget what a shocking impact Billie's sound and style had at the time, once she was on records. It was something completely new. And it wasn't to the general taste.   JOHN HAMMOND

People didn't dig it, same as people didn't dig Lester's sound at first. But I would tell her, 'Don't you change.'   ROY ELDRIDGE

She never had a really big voice – it was small, like a bell, that rang and went a mile.   BARNEY JOSEPHSON

It was a voice with what I would call a cutting edge.   MILT GABLER

It was a *sound* that fit the style she was singing. If Lady'd had a voice like Sarah Vaughan or Ella Fitzgerald, it wouldn't work.   BOBBY TUCKER

It would give you the goose pimples when you heard it. It gave you the chills up and down your arms, you know. At least, I always got them. I always got them.   BARBARA CARROLL

Lady was almost crude in her singing – but beautiful.   BOBBY TUCKER

Sometimes I think she'd wake up and not *have* a voice, you know. But she'd *sing*, anyway. I never heard her try for anything she didn't make.   MAL WALDRON

Billie Holiday could make you feel everything she was feeling. Whatever she was feeling. There's few singers can do that, you know.   SHIRLEY HORN

You know, there's nothing more embarrassing than someone *emoting* to you. But Billie can sing a line like, 'It's a heartache, anyway' out of 'But Beautiful', or she says 'Tomorrow was made for some' in 'For All We Know' and you just burst into tears. She just *says* those words, and it's so moving.   RICHARD RODNEY BENNETT

You could talk to her off the stand and hardly understand her, but, when she sang, you could not only understand, you could *feel* what she meant.   BOBBY TUCKER

She could make music out of talking.   BERYL BRYDEN

She made music out of speech, or speech out of music, it's hard to separate the two.   SHIRLEY HORN

Billie Holiday had a way of telling a story. All a singer is doing is telling a story to music.   CLEO LAINE

She never thought too much of herself as a singer, anyway. She thought of herself more as an extension of a jazz horn. She liked Louis and Pres and she more or less tried to phrase her singing to the way they would play.   BOBBY TUCKER

She was a singer most musicians liked. I don't know if they considered her one of the fellas, but there was something about her that they liked. And there are not too many singers that musicians like.

The way she sang was just totally in tune with her generation of jazz musicians. CARRIE SMITH

We never thought Lady would come out to California, but she did. I stood at the back of the club, little punk piano player of twenty-two, and by the end of the first night I was in love with her. Sure was. Stayed that way, too. I loved playing for her. It was *rare*. She was something else, that girl. Poor girl. JIMMY ROWLES

It wasn't like playing for a singer, it was like playing for another horn. Because she responded to everything like a jazz musician. MAL WALDRON

She was part of the music. That's why everybody loved her. She wasn't just a singer. She was *there*. JIMMY ROWLES

No question about it, she actually *heard* it, the music. Oh, she was a great listener. She could always listen. BOBBY TUCKER

She never learned to read music, she never studied music. And the notes she sang were a natural choice within her scope. But she was *right*, she was a natural musician. She was a natural talent. MAL WALDRON

Natural ability is a rarity. People who start out with natural good timing, good taste, the natural ability to affect an audience, these people are rare. BETTY CARTER

She didn't believe her gift, she didn't. She used to laugh. We'd get good reviews and she'd laugh. She wasn't really aware of what she had, this God-given talent that made her so unusual. BILL DILLARD

She didn't have *time* to study, she didn't have time for it, you see. It takes time to go to school; it takes time *away* from living the life that you're living which is really responsible for the music you're singing. MAL WALDRON

Billie's singing was from a *need*. SHEILA JORDAN

I played for her when she was at her peak in the forties. And I knew her before, when she was around fifteen, up in Harlem, you know. Yes, yes, she was a big laughing girl in those days. And a beautiful girl, of course. She was a lovely-looking girl. TRUMMY YOUNG

She could look wonderful, and she was attractive to men in a most destructive way. MAL WALDRON

157

When you're that young and you're around the scene, everything appeals to you. And you appeal to the wrong people too.   CARRIE SMITH

To tell you the truth I was a little afraid of her. We were almost the same age, but Billie thought I was a square. And she could never understand why I didn't make a pass at her. But I was a very straight young man in those days. I didn't smoke, or drink, or lust very much.   JOHN HAMMOND

She was singing well but nobody knew her. She hated going round and picking up the money between her legs like some of them did. She wouldn't do it. That's why they called her 'Lady'. You did it her way, or forget it. We all respected her for that, you know.   TRUMMY YOUNG

It's quite possible that she had seen everything by that young age. By the age of seventeen she had experienced a lot of life. So if she had to sing a sad song she didn't have to imagine how it felt to be hurt, to be lonely, to have somebody leave you or mistreat you.   BILL DILLARD

With Billie, the things she went through came out in her singing.   BARBARA JAY

We read things into it, years later.   BILL DILLARD

It's how you *transform* your experiences that's important.   MAGGIE NICOLS

Of course, when she started out, she was a scared young kid. Then she learned to cover it up. But there was always the tender part beneath, which was there.   MAL WALDRON

I saw some TV clips with some beautiful close-up things of Billie and you could see this *gentle* quality, overlaid with the brittle exterior. But you can't fool television, it gets right underneath, and you could see the gentleness in her eyes. Like the eyes of deer – they're shy, and yet they're direct – her eyes were just like that.   MARK MURPHY

Vulnerable? Oh, like a *child* . . .   BOBBY TUCKER

She had a beautiful personality, except when she started cursing, she could *curse*. Yes, she could be very fiery at times.   JULIA STEELE

158

You should have seen her when she'd get up and at 'em. She was Joe Louis. And with her old man, she was like a little *baby*. He used to beat her up and all. I was scared to death of him, everybody was.   JIMMY ROWLES

It seemed to me that she was pretty easy hurt. You could hurt her very easy, it seemed to me. And people took advantage of her, you know.   MAL WALDRON

She definitely acquired a manner – that dignity, and the way she could control an audience when she was at her best. She was the first non-white singer to sing with Artie Shaw's band, and also with Paul Whiteman. He was supposedly King of Jazz at the time. But to have one of the great black stars singing with your band wasn't acceptable. It was acceptable to go to Harlem and see black groups. It wasn't acceptable to go to a smart hotel and see black players.   BOBBY TUCKER

When a woman like Billie Holiday was standing on stage in front of the Artie Shaw band, and she and Artie were together and riding in the same car together, when she couldn't have a drink with him at the bar in the place they're both working, and she couldn't walk into the front door of the place, I think this all had a strong effect on her psychologically.   ROSETTA REITZ

She wasn't a bad girl. More like a nice soft piece of clay – she could be moulded, pushed one way or the other depending on her environment. She had to stand so much she got moulded wrong.   BARNEY JOSEPHSON

She was exploited in so many ways, all her life. Her emotions were exploited along with everything in her professional life. I didn't know her when she was very young. But, hearing talk, I figured that she must have been very, very vulnerable out there, at that young age.   MAL WALDRON

★

I saw the possibilities of the juke box market, and I went to see the head of the American Record Company. The company was already turning out routine versions of pop tunes. So I said, 'Why not use black musicians for the juke box market?' He decided to take a gamble. So Brunswick signed Teddy Wilson at a hundred dollars a week to do a series of sides. And I used Billie as a vocalist.   JOHN HAMMOND

I got seventy-five dollars a day for the sessions. And for that I hired a band, picked the tunes, rehearsed Billie and sketched out the arrangements, such as they were. All the sidemen – Johnny Hodges, Lester Young, Chu Berry, Roy Eldridge, Gene Krupa, Benny Goodman – got twenty dollars apiece. Billie got fifty dollars. We'd do four tunes in three hours. In those days, most of us were broke and hungry. We were glad to get on records, and whatever they paid us was all right.   TEDDY WILSON

No one really liked Billie's singing and the song pluggers hated it when they heard what the musicians did with the dog tunes the publishers let us have. Then 'I Cried for You' put Billie on the map. And in January 1937, I started recording the Basie guys with Teddy and Billie and I'll never forget that very first time. The electricity between Jo Jones, Buck Clayton, Billie and Lester was just fantastic.   JOHN HAMMOND

Musicians would almost fight to be on a Billie session, because they loved what she did. And they knew they could contribute something to it. Gosh, to get to play eight bars behind Billie – that's something they hoped for – to play something that made Billie sing *better*. They knew it would be an important record session.   MILT GABLER

People talk about the liberties Billie took with tunes. She didn't take liberties at all with the words, and the liberties she took with the melody were towards simplifying rather than making it more complex. She would smooth out a line, rather than make it into some acrobatic vocal exercise. This is more intriguing to me, more musical, than all kinds of swoops and moans and vocal tricks. Billie never resorted to that, and neither did Louis Armstrong. They both *edited* their songs extemporaneously.   DAVE FRISHBERG

When she took up a tune, she felt it the way a jazz musician would. She'd get the piano player to play it down a few times, and she'd listen to the tune, and she'd get an overall approach to the tune, and she sang it as a *whole*. She didn't work on it bar by bar, the way most singers do. Jazz musicians think of a tune in terms of a unit, a sequence, how it moves; you have to, if you're going to solo on it. That's how she heard a tune.   MAL WALDRON

I don't think I ever sing the same way twice. I don't think I ever sing the same tempo. One night it's a little bit slower, next night it's a little bit brighter, according to how I feel.   BILLIE HOLIDAY

There's a sort of way that singers take over songs. Not to use them as vehicles, exactly, but to make a personal expression out of them. And this is what Billie did. And this was her genius for taking songs that weren't actually very good and just breaking you up with them.   RICHARD RODNEY BENNETT

A lot of her songs didn't have too much content, but she could find gold in them.   BERYL BRYDEN

A lot of these songs had to have Billie to be remembered at all.   DIGBY FAIRWEATHER

As she sang a new song, each night she would find different ways of bending a note here and there, and she'd do it the next night, and that's how it would develop and grow.   MAL WALDRON

As far as we know, Billie Holiday never shoobeedoo-ed. She stuck to the words. But she always surrounded herself with jazzmen, and she made sure they had a voice.   BOB DOROUGH

She might do songs that didn't suit her on records sometimes, but her actual performance was very personal, and she only sang what she liked. It was a different thing altogether. People would come up and ask her for things off records, and she'd look at them and say, 'I don't have it on this set.'   SLIM GAILLARD

Everything I *do* sing is part of my life.   BILLIE HOLIDAY

But she didn't become a star until I did my first records with her and they were successful. The Commodore recording of 'Strange Fruit' and 'Fine and Mellow' was a turning-point in her career as a popular artist, rather than just a jazz singer that John Hammond used on the Teddy Wilson recordings. I told her to go and ask John Hammond to ask the company to let her record 'Strange Fruit' for me. They didn't want to risk making it because of the record dealers in the southern parts of the United States. 'Strange Fruit' was a very strong protest song, and the public took note of her, and went to hear her sing it. But, you know, the real hit side was 'Fine and Mellow', the blues that we threw together on the back. That's the song that made Billie Holiday popular.   MILT GABLER

★

By 1945, the happenings had all moved to 52nd Street. Coleman Hawkins and Lady Day were the King and Queen.   BABS GONZALES

Generally the 52nd Street nightclubs were small places, dark, smokey. And all you'd see was the head of the singer in a little pin spot.   MILT GABLER

She'd walk up to the microphone real slow, and she had one of the happiest smiles anybody could see, and she'd look at people real pleasant. And she'd just *melt* the audience with her personality. She was so *welcomed*. She just walked out there nice and slow, and she'd stand there and look. And smile. And the piano or the group would wait until she'd say she was ready, and then she'd go into her song. She didn't do any of those cheap things singers do, no no no no no, she didn't need to. She just sang.   SLIM GAILLARD

You know the way singers shake their asses now. Billie didn't have to do that. Her mouth was so sensuous: she was pretty and she would say certain words and her mouth would quiver and she always had this white gardenia and long gloves.   MILES DAVIS

I couldn't believe how *sexy* Billie Holiday was, until I saw the TV stuff on her. She was so *hot*. She had such an overwhelming sexuality, I was quite, you know, shocked. She didn't have to do anything, it was just *there*. They must have had to restrain some of the guys in the audience.   MARK MURPHY

She was like a queen, like a beautiful African queen to me, the way she held her head, when she sang.   MILT GABLER

Yes, audiences would cry, right there in front of her, sometimes, she moved them so much. I never knew her mind, but I don't think she was *torching*, it didn't seem that way. It seemed to me that she felt she was just trying to please the audience, plus trying to make herself happy by pleasing the audience.   SLIM GAILLARD

It was all internal, wasn't it? It was her concentration that could *get* the whole place. It's remarkable she could hang on to that regardless of what was going on in her life.   ROSEMARY CLOONEY

She was *real* in front of the audience.   SLIM GAILLARD

She just came out and sang. And if they made too much noise, she'd walk off. She didn't care. If you didn't like her, she'd go home.   TRUMMY YOUNG

When Billie Holiday was with me at the Café Society, her vice was marijuana. I told them they'd all be fired if they brought it near the club. So every night between shows, she'd be driven round and round Central Park in a hackney smoking one goddamn reefer after another. One night she came back and I could tell from her eyes that she was really high. She finished her first number and maybe she didn't like the way the audience reacted. Singers often wore just gown and slippers, no underwear, because it's pretty warm under the lights. And Billie just turned her back, bent over, flipped up her gown and walked off the floor.   BARNEY JOSEPHSON

She'd always come down in the morning and smile, 'Hey, Slim, what you doing?' 'Oh, just sitting around, looking at the ocean out there.' We were staying in the same place in San Francisco, and it looked on the ocean. She'd take a little walk, and later she'd come on back and get her rest for the night's work. And she'd get all polished up for her work. She would take a great time to ready. And then she would walk out on that stage, and people would just love her.   SLIM GAILLARD

For the five years that Billie Holiday worked for me at Kelly's Stables, she was a doll. I never had a bit of trouble with her. When I came back from overseas, she was a changed girl. Before that, the worst thing she ever did was to smoke pot. Everyone did. It wasn't a crime, as it is now. Somehow along the line she got married and I think that's where the problem started. That's what I heard anyway. When I saw her after the war, she was on a very expensive habit.
RALPH WATKINS

She sang like an angel not because of it, but despite it. What could any of us do?   BARNEY JOSEPHSON

After she became the great Lady Day, it seems to me it all happened for her so suddenly, she just couldn't handle it.   BILL DILLARD

Billie Holiday was known, known, known.   MAXINE SULLIVAN

See, when you become a big singer, a big performer, there are so many people in the street who are out to entice you into some evil activity, for their own personal gains, so that they can control you. If you are hooked, you can't function unless they are providing you.   BILL DILLARD

Soon as you get a nice little gig, look like you'll make some money, there's a guy right *there*, waiting to hook you.   JULIA STEELE

She just enjoyed living, and she wanted to enjoy living. *But* you have to take care of your physical condition. Nobody in the street is going to take care of your voice. If you're at a party and they encourage you to sniff a little coke or become involved in something to be *sociable*, if you're tired, *you* have to say, 'I'm going.' And really *go*.   BILL DILLARD

When you're young, you're not into things. It's when you become a little disappointed that you go into things more. It takes an amount of foolishness or disappointment to start dissipating.   HELEN MERRILL

She didn't care as long as she felt good and could hang out with her friends and get loaded. She surrounded herself with not the tastiest of people.   ANNIE ROSS

Heroin makes strange friends.   ANITA O'DAY

There were so many people interested in keeping her subjugated. Teddy Wilson told me that before she got into those circles, the musicians used to take care of her, and when she was with musicians, she was fine. It was when she got into the other circles of flattery, she went the way of all flesh.   HELEN MERRILL

And, in the end, most of the musicians had deserted her. Yes, perhaps they despaired of her.   ANNIE ROSS

Nobody understood that part. I know I didn't. Bad taste in men friends? Oh, the *worst*. But she wanted to do what she wanted to do. And nobody could tell her what to do. This is how she lived.   TRUMMY YOUNG

She was married to Jimmy Monroe. But there was a period when we went into Club Ebony, and one of the managers, one of the owners I guess, he just moved in and *took her over*. But it was all self-seeking. For *him*. Oh, she could pick 'em all right. She was attracted to that kind of person. Don't ask me why.   BOBBY TUCKER

Billie was with a man who took all her money. He'd, like, give her ten dollars. And turn down jobs because there wasn't enough money for him to steal. I don't know if they're in *love* with these people, but he is, like, *her man*. And he can do whatever he wants.   JIMMY ROWLES

Maybe she wasn't sure of her love-life, but she sure was sure of her singing.   HELEN HUMES

Yes, often singing was the only thing that could go right for her. Her moods would affect the music, of course. When she wasn't feeling too well, we'd play mostly blues tunes. And when she was feeling very good, we'd play happy tunes. Because she only sang what she

164

felt. What she felt like singing at that moment.   MAL WALDRON

Oh, Lady loved torch songs. When I first worked with her, when she first came to California, we used to do all kinds of tunes, up tunes, medium tunes. The older she got I think the more she liked the pretty, slow ones – 'I'll Be Seeing You', stuff like that. Because she was having a few bad affairs. And she just got to where she liked to sing those kind of songs. She was probably thinking about her old man or something. Or one of her old men. She had a lot of boyfriends. And a couple of them were kind of rough.   JIMMY ROWLES

From what I've heard – I never knew her – when Billie sang those masochistic love songs, those torch songs, she was but recounting episodes of her life. So it was truthful for her.   GRADY TATE

She identified with words very strongly, and if the words told her own story, then she was very strongly attracted to the tune.   MAL WALDRON

I think Billie Holiday could find the *sense* of a song underneath it. Like 'When You're Smiling' – it's a platitude, 'When you're smiling the whole world smiles with you'. But when you think about it, it's *true*, irony apart, that what you put out is what you get back. She could always pinpoint the reality of a song, the reality behind the platitude, behind the frivolity. It's more than just singing a melody or a chord or a style, you know. And it's not an intellectual process, either, it's *living*. It's living your life. It's not something you can do if you've been protected. That kind of optimism comes out of coming through against horrendous odds.   JEANNE LEE

People who are oppressed are often hipper than their oppressors.
MAGGIE NICOLS

I think she got caught up in that tragedy queen image. She became less of the natural performer she had been.   BILL DILLARD

Audiences can be greedy. And destructive. She wasn't a tragedy queen, but she, kind of, became one.   ANNIE ROSS

When you find something that really gets your audience, you do it. And you can get caught up in your own act, in a way. When she was a girl she was doing lighthearted things more. When she did 'Strange Fruit', I'm sure it had a lot of effect on her.   MAXINE SULLIVAN

I insisted she closed every show with it every night. Lights out, just one small spinlight, and all service stopped. I was doing agitprop, see. To me it was a piece of propaganda. There were no encores after it. My instruction was walk off, period. People had to remember 'Strange Fruit', get their insides burned with it.   BARNEY JOSEPHSON

And, in the end, when she didn't have the energy or the strength left, she copied her own singing. She was more or less a parasite to herself.   HELEN MERRILL

And then a lot of people would come to look at her because they'd figure she was doped up, that sort of thing. And she was a notorious person, to a lot of people.   SLIM GAILLARD

She was a *target*.   JIMMY ROWLES

The vice-squad would come round and sit around in the audience and look at her, watch her, see where she's going and when she leaves and who with and what she's doing.   SLIM GAILLARD

When Billie Holiday got busted in the forties, when she went to jail, it was headlines in the papers. You didn't hear so much when Anita O'Day got busted, or how many times. There were no rehabilitation places for black people, only prison.   BETTY CARTER

The very place where she could have worked successfully for all time was New York City. And, because she'd been arrested, she could not get the permit that was necessary to work wherever they sold liquor. So she just couldn't work. This may have had something to do with her despair.   BARBARA CARROLL

She went along with the tide. Billie Holiday did so little to help her own singing career. John Hammond found her and from that she began to grow. She never studied singing. She couldn't read music. She didn't do anything to help herself. She rode along with what had already been promoted for her. When it all comes easy, you don't know what you have, and you're not prepared to protect it from these outside forces that will pressure you.   BILL DILLARD

Talk about covering up for her . . . The last couple of years she was with Decca, we recorded her with orchestras. Billie would come in, and till she opened her throat – I always had a bottle of brandy for her – I would rehearse the band and get the whole thing balanced. Because she was what I call a one-take artist. I'd run it down once, to get a level and see if she was reading the words right, and then go for it on the next take. And, very often that would be the one. And I'd do all the sides in forty-five minutes, because after that her throat would close up again and I'd have to send the band home.

166

The company never knew I was recording her in forty-five minutes when she was booked for three hours, and getting high on record dates. MILT GABLER

Billie never done anything to anybody but herself. Because she was a lovely person, but when you're addicted to something, then what else? What else is there? HELEN HUMES

It was kicks, from drinking and marijuana, and then the drugs. Even after she was sent to the hospital, she went back to the drugs when she came out. *She wanted it.* MILT GABLER

If you were a drug addict, you were a criminal. If she'd stayed in Europe, the need for it would have gone away, I think. Like it did for me, because I got involved in all that stuff too. MAL WALDRON

Billie is my oldest daughter's godmother. The last date she had in California, I was pregnant with my second child. And she looked at me and said, 'I think you have a girl child in your belly this time. And I think I should be her godmother, because it takes a very bad woman to be a good godmother.' ROSEMARY CLOONEY

I saw Billie Holiday live just one time. I was going to have my baby. I was almost in labour. And my mother said, 'It's crazy, you shouldn't go.' And I said, 'I'm going to have the baby *later*.' I don't know what she was feeling, but it was so intense it was frightening. Whatever the feeling was, it stayed with me all week. I don't think she sang more than four or five songs that night. She interpreted the lyric as if it had just happened to her. She was really sick when I saw her, and that kind of hurt me. I remembered the stories about her. I cried. SHIRLEY HORN

We did a show once, it was a benefit, and as usual she was unprepared. She didn't want to do it. She sang 'My Man'. And she was, like, under the influence, her eyes started to run. And the people thought, *tears.* And the people were crying, the engineers were crying. And when she came off she was furious that it, you know, *showed.* BOBBY TUCKER

A lot of people tell me that they love Billie Holiday's late product. I don't even listen to it, that stuff she did with Ray Ellis, even though many musicians I respect rave about it. 'Lady in Satin', that aspect of Billie Holiday, doesn't interest me. Nor does it reach me. I really like the young musician Billie Holiday. DAVE FRISHBERG

I loved 'Lady in Satin'. It told a lot about her life, about her loves, her emotional ups and downs, what she had been through.   MAX ROACH

'Lady in Satin' is so moving, the flaws, the vulnerability. Somehow, a really perfect voice, a really perfect technique is a sort of shell. It's a kind of armour that comes between me and the song.   RICHARD RODNEY BENNETT

With Billie Holiday, if the voice wasn't there, another sound was there to express what she wanted to express.   JAY CLAYTON

As her range got less, her expressiveness within the range was even more. She compensated for the fact that the mechanism was diminishing, by the breathtaking emotion that she was able to project. And that was always the thing with Billie. She made you feel something.   BARBARA CARROLL

If there is such a thing as a jazz singer, Billie Holiday *is*.   ABBEY LINCOLN

She sang jazz. She was jazz, herself. Not many singers can sing jazz.   TRUMMY YOUNG

When she sang something, it touched a universal button.   HELEN MERRILL

It always surprised me to hear people say how much influence Billie Holiday had on them. We worked for a year in one of the clubs on 52nd Street, that, when, *if*, it was jam-packed, would have held about ninety-eight people. You know, she did well, but very rarely was it packed, except at weekends. Everybody's got wise after the event. When she was alive, nobody bothered very much.   BOBBY TUCKER

In her heyday, she always made enough money – not like the superstars now, of course. But Joe Glaser, her manager, told me at one time, 'She's making five thousand dollars a week now. And she's always broke.' Either her men took the money away from her. Or the pushers.   MILT GABLER

It was like Lester Young, seeing everybody *else* get rich on your style.   BOBBY TUCKER

I often think of Billie Holiday and Lester Young in tandem. As a phenomenon, the two of them. And I think if you look at their recorded output, and the pattern and shape of their lives, they

168

paralleled each other, right downhill. From the very first records they made, to the last. Their records got worse and worse, that's my opinion. The greatest product they ever turned out was in the beginning. And their tones changed in kind. Their tones went from bright, rhythmic and vital, to dead, deadpan, maudlin. Billie's singing at the end sounds just like Lester's playing at the end. And vice versa. It's as if the two of them were bit by the same bug and went down together.   DAVE FRISHBERG

I took some pictures of her the last time she was in London, the year she died. She looked very, very beautiful, but she was painfully thin. You could see she was really quite a big lady who'd shrunk. She had that lovely smile and she could get it together for the show, but when she was relaxed, all the sadness shows. I won't have those sad pictures published.   BERYL BRYDEN

The last time she was in London she used to come into the club where I was playing piano. And she'd pull up a chair beside me, and put her arms round my neck and put her head on my shoulder and sing like that all night. All she wanted to do was sing. And sometimes she'd cry.   ALAN CLARE

I came back to New York and Lady Day had lost her voice. She was very lonely because all her jive friends wouldn't visit her fearing they'd have to give her some bread. I took her to Lester Young's funeral and about four months later she went to the hospital never to come out alive again.   BABS GONZALES

And you know they arrested her on her death bed.   ANNIE ROSS

She had a lot. She had an awful lot. She had so much that people are still living off it.   JEANNE LEE

In New York you can still hear three or four 'Billie Holidays' a night.   JOY KANE

But so many singers copy the mannerisms, rather than the essence, the musicality.   ABBEY LINCOLN

You can't do anything about becoming *her*. A lot of singers tried. And a lot went into drugs and things, thinking that's what would make them sing better.   HELEN MERRILL

Some people are influenced, and some are out-and-out thieves. And do it very successfully. There were some straight down-the-line out-and-out copyists trying to copy her feeling and style. And the

one who received the least reward was Billie Holiday.   BOBBY
TUCKER

I was in her presence twice and the second was at a party given for
her in Philadelphia. She was going downhill then. She didn't look
like the Billie I knew, the radiant young Billie I remembered, with
the gardenia in her hair. And it ended up with them making her pay
for it, the party. They gave her this party. And stuck her with the
tab.   JULIA STEELE

10
Why?

There's all kinds of singers, that's for sure.   CHET BAKER

Singers have been part of jazz from earliest times. And it seems to have gone – that whole mystique about who was or wasn't a jazz singer which was so boring.   RICHARD RODNEY BENNETT

I don't know what a jazz singer is, but then nobody has yet defined *jazz*.   DIGBY FAIRWEATHER

They characterize Lady as a jazz singer. What is a jazz singer? Does that mean you're supposed to do a lot of scat singing? Or is it the type of *song* you sing?   BOBBY TUCKER

You can sing any type of song and make it a jazz song.   SALENA JONES

There's no such thing as a jazz singer. And that includes all of us. We are all jazz-influenced singers. Every American singer is a jazz-influenced singer, because it's our native folk art.   MEL TORME

I'm a jazz singer, no doubt about it. And I know it. I don't try to avoid that label, like a lot of people do. If I say, 'I'm a singer', you wouldn't get nothing from that. But if I say, 'I'm a *jazz* singer . . .'   BETTY CARTER

I prefer to say, 'I'm an improviser'. For me the art of improvisation is it. I prefer not to call it jazz or anything as people can be very

171

argumentative. But you can't argue with improvisation.   BOBBY McFERRIN

Being a jazz stylist, I never do the song the same way twice.   ANITA O'DAY

I was at a jazz vocalists' festival in Czechoslovakia, and there was only one other Dixieland singer, in my style. But the guys ranged from copies of Ray Charles and rare old blue singers, all taken off records they'd managed to get, to one guy who was making sounds into a Moog synthesizer. And there were a lot of scat singers, either out of Ella, or the more way-out Karin Krog school.   BERYL BRYDEN

I know some great singers who can't sing jazz. It isn't something you can learn. Jazz is a feel. It's what comes from inside. You can sing anything, a pop tune, and a jazz flavour is in it. And another person can sing the song and it may be beautiful but the jazz flavour isn't there. It's a certain rhythm and a certain timbre in your voice. It's difficult to explain. Someone could sing the same notes as a jazz singer sang, and it wouldn't come out jazz.   TRUMMY YOUNG

I feel honoured if they call my music jazz. I'm honoured because I think jazz is one of the most difficult forms of music, requiring skill, training, understanding, feeling and respect from other musicians who recognize you as a jazz musician.   FLORA PURIM

I think it's possible for a singer to be a jazz musician. I think someone like Betty Carter *is* a jazz musician, with an exceptional musical talent. Singers have possibly the best instrument of all, the voice.   PAT SMYTHE

Some singers are really into the world of sound, and the voice as an instrument.   BOB DOROUGH

I believe in the music of the moment. Happening one time, and that's it. There is such an incredible beauty in doing something just once.   BOBBY McFERRIN

All over the place, I imagine people must be experimenting a bit, I'm sure more people must be doing it. But you don't really hear an improvising singer on records or on the radio too much. Perhaps people tend to give up before they've got very far with it.   NORMA WINSTONE

I didn't start to improvise because I thought, ooh, I'm going to come up with something new. It came out of a long evolution. Which started with the basic material that was over here. JEANNE LEE

It's supposed to be very spontaneous. I know that when I improvise the scatting is always different. Improvisation is about taste, it's about what you're feeling about this particular song. And it's also about the ability of your musicians to do certain things with the music to make it interesting to you so that you *can* improvise with taste. What they play behind you feeds information to your brain. That's what jazz is all about.   BETTY CARTER

Jazz is an art which is based on improvisation. But not improvisation as just *freedom*, but disciplines applied to the expression – the disciplines of rhythm and tonality and harmony. And the disciplines of being able to work with someone else, without cutting the other ideas off in order to put your own down. Jazz is an incredible life process.   JEANNE LEE

Though I'm doing a lot of improvising, I don't like to change a song just to be clever. I like to feel a song changes through an emotional colour or inflection, or sometimes just by the way you bend a note because suddenly that's how you feel. It's an intuitive thing.
MAGGIE NICOLS

I don't take these chances because I'm saying, 'I want to be different.' The important thing is, first, singing what you feel. I think it's important to have your music honest. And to maintain your own sound. To copy somebody else's sound doesn't make you a jazz singer; you're just an imitation. Then, you try to communicate with what's happening with the rest of the musicians. Because they feed you and in turn you feed them, if something musical is happening.   SHEILA JORDAN

I didn't want to just do the tune. I kept hearing these . . . things. And I wanted to go further. You start to hear things. You hear form. You understand choruses going by. The harmony becomes part of you, whether you sing the roots of the chords or not. You learn. So, if you have that urge, and you must have it, it starts to inspire you, lines, melodies, rhythms.   JAY CLAYTON

Like, you *start*. You start because you feel something personal. That's your genesis. But you have to underlay that with knowledge of the tradition, so you have something to go from, some continuity or some meaning, and then you take it *out* from there.
JEANNE LEE

I take off on improvised solos. Sometimes it upsets people. They think I'm mad. Or, 'What is she doing, that sound?' It's something that I feel. It's something that I really can't control. And I'm feeling it more strongly as I grow older. These things that come out and the feeling I'm feeling, not holding back, it makes the sounds seem OK, when they come out. And maybe technically it *is* wrong. And maybe it *is* different. And maybe you're *not* used to hearing it.   SHEILA JORDAN

If you're experimenting, every area has its own risks.   MAGGIE NICOLS

First thoughts are best. The spontaneous thing is always better to me. You have to be *good*, sure, to be spontaneous and good.   MILT JACKSON

Mistakes are a precious quality in improvising to me. Because it's how you get out of and transform mistakes that's exciting. It's the risks. It's actually trying for things, that takes you beyond somebody that's just competent.   MAGGIE NICOLS

Anything too perfect is sterile.   LEON THOMAS

That's why you train yourself to go for the moment. It's in the music – you must be into *change*. When you're young, you're kind of scared to *go* with that instinct. You get the instinct, you always *know* but it's a question of will – to *believe* what you know.   JAY CLAYTON

I went up to the Little Theatre Club, this tiny little place, with about five people in the audience. And I heard Norma, Kenny Wheeler, Trevor Watts, John Stevens and the others. And I thought, how do they *do* this? It seemed so complex and intricate and strange and free. But I could *hear* a voice in it. I spoke to John after and he said, 'Come up and sing.' But I was too nervous. And then I got pissed with Trevor Watts at some press do, and I suppose I was bolder, so I went. And John just said, 'Right, here's what we're going to do. Take a breath and sing the first note that comes into your head. And just keep repeating that note.' And I was so nervous and my voice was wobbling. And at the same time he did a thing with a gong, and Trevor played another note. And after a while the note became just like breathing out and I forgot about being nervous. And before I knew where I was, the whole thing had turned into a beautiful improvisation. And I'd never experienced anything like it in my *life*. I was *high*. I came out of the Little Theatre Club and I rushed over to the Venus Rooms, this strip joint, where I was singing for a

174

pittance. And in the end I just blew the gig at the Venus Rooms, because I kept going up to the Theatre Club. And so I joined the Spontaneous Music Ensemble. I was invited into this amazing world. And for a while I didn't want to sound remotely like anything to do with songs. And I was afraid to use even consonants, let alone *words*, because this music was so different.   MAGGIE NICOLS

I suppose the first *sheer* bit of improvisation I did was with John at the Shakespeare Festival at Southwark Cathedral. We just did this free bit together. Michael Gibbs was supposed to bring the band in, but he just stood there, listening. And we went on and on, but he wouldn't bring the band in. Well, it was supposed to be Ophelia going mad, or something, so . . .   NORMA WINSTONE

When you're doing free stuff, you're all you've got.   JAY CLAYTON

The voice is endless.   BOBBY McFERRIN

I just hear so many things. If someone suggests something in a melody or harmony, I'm open to it. It touches a place in me that makes me want to extend what they are doing.   JEANNE LEE

I sang free music when it wasn't the vogue to be free. The musicians who invited me to sing were free players. So I've been involved in just about every type of jazz music, from bebop to free.   SHEILA JORDAN

Free is easy. I do free stuff on tunes just to let people know it's easy to do.   PETTY CARTER

The more freedom you have, the more responsibility you have.   JEANNE LEE

In my solo shows, I improvise words and lyrics and sometimes I just own up about something I'm thinking or feeling. I quote from my past. And I mix it with lyrical stuff and angry stuff.   MAGGIE NICOLS

There's something so fascinating to me about standing on the stage all by myself and just singing. Singing that music that just comes to me at the moment, and never happens again. I want to do that more than anything in the world.   BOBBY McFERRIN

I improvise every night. It depends on the way I feel, but I know when I do a certain sound, the music will come down, when I want to bring it down. It's like a musical understanding: that whoever makes the strongest statement *leads*. I feel that if I go in there and break down what's happening – with this *sound* – I have something to say. And they come down, very respectfully, musically, dynamically, and let me say it. So then I say what I *threaten* to say. Is that understandable?   FLORA PURIM

There are sections in my music that are completely, totally improvised, open, free. Usually at the beginning or the end of the song. At the beginning the musicians are playing just whatever we feel at the moment, and I'm setting up the song, half talking, half singing, a lot of free association. That's the attitude the band has – half playing in time, half without time, just doing what you feel and trying to feel it together. So we can create this mood together. And then the song happens.   AL JARREAU

Sometimes I hear the sound coming from me and I know I am not really controlling it. It's like being a medium. It uses me. And it's possible because, and only if, you can clear away all the rubbish that stands in the way of this happening.   ABBEY LINCOLN

You can make any sound, and you *choose*, but it's not a conscious choice. It's interesting to see how one sound leads to another.   BOBBY McFERRIN

A lot of people don't realize that a great deal of what we do comes *through* us, as opposed to us doing it so much. So you prepare for this. And you study your craft. And what happens will come through you.   JOE WILLIAMS

There's a sort of intellectual part that you use. And an emotional and a spiritual part of you as well, that's all expressed through jazz. It's a very deep music. And, I mean it's limitless.   JULIE AMIET

It's madness actually. I think I'm just trying to show the madness that's in us all. And the madness that's repressed, that ends up being distorted by authority, by the system, and controlled by drugs, and all that.   MAGGIE NICOLS

When you've lasted as long as we all have, you must have valleys and peaks. And I believe talent rests, sometimes. Sometimes it just stops. And you have to stop. And then it slowly comes back again.   HELEN MERRILL

And, you know, maturing goes on, whether you're singing or not.   MARILYN MOORE

And the beautiful thing about jazz singing is that it knows no age.

176

The older you are and the longer you've been singing it, the better you become. Which is quite the opposite of a pop singer – your good looks go, or your voice goes, they don't want you any more. But in jazz, the older you get, the more authority you have. SHEILA JORDAN

I think maybe now my time has come. Maybe I can handle it better now than I could have twenty years ago. Things go in cycles and all the good singers are coming back. SHIRLEY HORN

I know I'm a legend, they call me a legend. I have to realize that. ADELAIDE HALL

You know, I tell 'em, 'There's still a little starch in the old girl yet.' MAXINE SULLIVAN

People say, 'Gee, you're seventy now, why do you keep doing it?' And I say, 'I never look back, somebody may be gaining on me.' BILL DILLARD

Music and laughter keeps you young. PETER DEAN

Now I'm sixty-six, but to me age doesn't mean a damn thing. My youngest son is twenty-six, *he* looks older than me. RAY ELLINGTON

Jazz allows you to sound fifty when you are fifty. When you are nineteen, you should sound nineteen. Jazz allows you to tell the truth – be what you are. MAX ROACH

Alberta Hunter is out singing again. She's eighty-eight now and she says she hasn't had so much fun in forty years. BOBBY TUCKER

For me, I don't think it would have made any difference, psychologically, if I'd become successful at twenty-two, instead of forty-two. But musically it's made a big difference. People have said I'm a fusion pioneer, and I guess it's true. It wasn't called that when I started out, I was just doing what I was doing. AL JARREAU

You get better. What else? We're always being told we're 'sophisticated' and in a way it bugs me, it's kind of derogatory. People don't seem to realize we've been working some thirty years. You perfect your craft. You get better and better. And then people call you 'slick'. Well, thanks a lot. JACKIE CAIN

And the other thing is to have patience in your own development, musically. There isn't any short cut. JAY CLAYTON

I know I'm oversensitive and I overreact and worry. I can be very easily hurt about my singing. I keep saying, 'Now, calm down.' But sensitivity makes an artist, so you try to use it for you not against you.   SUSANNAH McCORKLE

A laid back style, that's what I'm known for. And that's definitely not the way I am. Most performers try to achieve in their performance something they haven't achieved in their life.   MOSE ALLISON

I practise the arts, whether I'm being seen in public or not. I paint, I write poetry, I read it, I write, I do many things. Sometimes somebody will call me on the phone and it is an encouragement. Sometimes it is discouragement; that spirit of condemnation is here too. You have to survive that. And sometimes it's the mood you're in yourself; sometimes you interpret things in a negative way. It's like flying blind, a lot.   ABBEY LINCOLN

It's easy to get depressed. It's difficult to get un-depressed. You have to learn to carry these things with you patiently. I try to carry it as best I can.   BOBBY McFERRIN

★

Jazz is not just a hodge-podge, not just a new combination of other things. It really has its own aesthetic. It's as close as you can get to expressing what life is in the twentieth century.   JEANNE LEE

What is only just beginning to be explored, now that women are getting more chances to be creative, is the amazing richness of women's experience. And its diversity. And its shading. It was always said that women had limited experience, that they knew nothing of life. But, in their lives, women know the relation between concrete and abstract. Which is what we can give to total improvised music, because some men in the *avant garde* world get totally lost in the abstract. Now, women have always been aware of the intuitive, and when you're aware of the intuitive, you can develop it and make it work for you. Women have always been nurturers, and this has always been exploited, but it can be a creative force rather than a martyrdom. I have grown so much stronger since working with women musicians. I find more freshness, more enthusiasm, less cynicism among women musicians. But it doesn't mean that all those fears about male approval don't come up, because jazz is almost totally based on male standards. I mean, isn't it funny that it was supposed to be a compliment to say that Betty Smith 'played like a man'? Now I find myself thinking about singers like Al Jarreau, oh, he's not bad for a man. He's quite creative, for a man.   MAGGIE NICOLS

A lot of the stuff that's happening to me is kind of frightening in a way. It's all so new. Promotional things. Pressure from the record company and stuff. All I'm doing is singing. And I want to be ordinary and just sing.   BOBBY McFERRIN

I'm here to tell these singers that it isn't easy. I have two young students who are really quite talented and interested in jazz. They think it's hip to sing jazz. And they get so disgusted and depressed because they haven't made it. And these are kids in their early twenties. But once they get into the music and find out how much of a sacrifice you have to make to be able to do this kind of music and be true to yourself, they're easily brought down. And I tell them, 'If you feel that way, get out of it.'   JAY CLAYTON

Of course, everyone can sing, it's a natural act. They probably think that's all there is to it, really. Just practise a bit and there you are.   NORMA WINSTONE

Here's what you have to do. A lot of singers are reluctant to do the work; which means learning tunes because you love them, transposing them, calling musicians, understanding musicians, being scared, going to sit in, and, suddenly, you get a gig.   JAY CLAYTON

You have to do everything in the world to support the music, if it's not supporting you, to nourish it, to keep it pure. I've had a day-job all my life. And I don't expect too much, materially.   SHEILA JORDAN

My fortune is in my work. Even if it's stormy sometimes. And sometimes the sun shines. It's like the weather.   ABBEY LINCOLN

If you're going to get it, you're going to get it. It's going to come and get you and take you by the hand and say, 'Well, it's *your* turn.'   JULIA STEELE

When the opportunity presents itself, you must be qualified. It's a matter of preparing yourself for that. Be ready. Always have it in the back of your mind. And musicians will say, 'Hey, come up and sing something.'   JOE WILLIAMS

The process of creativity – how you work with your inner resources, how you bring your experiences and your situation to a point where you learn to synthesize it all creatively – that's quite a process. JEANNE LEE

It's almost like a prayer, really, singing jazz.   JULIE AMIET

That's the way this music *is*. If the Gods don't visit us on the stage, nothing happens. No matter how brilliant you are, a part of that brilliance is being about to call that God – the spirit of the music, that uses your body and expresses *itself*. That's the way it feels to me.   ABBEY LINCOLN

To me, to do music is like *Christmas*.   SHEILA JORDAN

I sing because I love to sing. I love to sing and to be happy. And if I can't make it feel like that, I'll go on home and play bingo, because I can be happy doing that, too.   HELEN HUMES

I say to myself, 'I love to sing. I was born to sing. I've been singing since I was a little kid. I might never open my mouth again.' So I treat every time I sing as if it could possibly be the last time.   SHEILA JORDAN

I sing and I play because that's what I *do*. If I stop playing and singing, I stop eating. I'm like a hamster. I get up. And the wheel is there. And I get on. Sometimes I hate it. And sometimes I don't hate it. But I know that if I don't do it for two or three days, I start to feel as if something is wrong.   BOBBY COLE

It's a different world when the music stops.   ANITA O'DAY

Vocabulary

Ad lib – out of tempo

Ballad – a song generally played at a slow tempo

Bridge – the 'middle eight' of a popular song

Busk, busking – playing without written music

Cans – earphones used in recording studios

Changes – the chord sequence of a piece of music

Chart – a musical arrangement

Chops – originally a player's embouchure, now applied to technique in general

Chorus – the unit of music to be played

Combo – a small group of musicians

Count it off – indicate the required tempo

Demo – a non-commercial record made to promote an artist, song or group

Dep – a replacement

Dots – written music

Down – depressing

Gig – a job

Intonation – in-tune-ness

Intro – the introduction to a song

Lick – a musical phrase

Medium groove – a tempo neither fast nor slow

Middle eight – the third eight bars in the usual thirty-two-bar song format

Passing – a black pretending to be a white

Release – the 'middle eight'

Root – the bottom note of a chord

Scatting – vocal improvisation without words

Set – a musical programme

Sitting in – informal and unpaid performance with a jazz group

Standard – a popular song which has stood the test of time

Top line – the melody line of a song

Index